COLORS & PATTERNS
of Depression Era
GLASSWARE

**Doris Yeske
and Lyle Fokken**

Schiffer
Publishing Ltd

4880 Lower Valley Road, Atglen, Pennsylvania 19310

Dedication

We dedicate this book to our families and friends, for without their continuous encouragement, enthusiasm, and support, this book would not be possible. It is also dedicated to all the workers and employees of America's Depression era glass houses whose skilled hands made the precious colored glass, which is so collectable today.

Schiffer Books are available at special discounts for bulk purchases for sales promotions or premiums. Special editions, including personalized covers, corporate imprints, and excerpts can be created in large quantities for special needs. For more information contact the publisher:

Published by Schiffer Publishing Ltd.
4880 Lower Valley Road
Atglen, PA 19310
Phone: (610) 593-1777; Fax: (610) 593-2002
E-mail: Info@schifferbooks.com

For the largest selection of fine reference books on this and related subjects, please visit our web site at **www.schifferbooks.com**
We are always looking for people to write books on new and related subjects. If you have an idea for a book please contact us at the above address.

This book may be purchased from the publisher.
Include $5.00 for shipping.
Please try your bookstore first.
You may write for a free catalog.

In Europe, Schiffer books are distributed by
Bushwood Books
6 Marksbury Ave.
Kew Gardens
Surrey TW9 4JF England
Phone: 44 (0) 20 8392 8585; Fax: 44 (0) 20 8392 9876
E-mail: info@bushwoodbooks.co.uk
Website: www.bushwoodbooks.co.uk

Designed by Mark David Bowyer
Type set in Zurich BT

ISBN: 978-0-76423-3422-1
Printed in China

Contents

Acknowledgments.................................4

Reflections 5

Introduction 6
    Price Guidelines..............................6

1: **Pink,** The Classic Color 7
2: **Green**, A Vibrant and Refreshing Color 30
3: **Yellow**, A Golden Topaz..................... 48
4: **Opalescent**, Tones of Opal Gemstone 59
5: **Cobalt Blue,** The Mystique Color............... 72
6: **Amber**, A Golden Brown Color 81
7: **Amethyst**, A Rich Purple Color 89
8: **Black,** A Dark Ebony 95
9: **Teal**, A Dark Blue Green............................ 106
10: **Iridescent**, A Lustrous Rainbow 112
11: **Jadite**, The Opaque Green 120
12: **Crystal**, A Colorless Glass 126
13: **Sky Blue**, A Light Blue 139
14: **Forest Green**, The Emerald Color 148
15: **Ruby Red**, A Festive Color........................ 154
16: **Milk Glass**, An Opaque White................. 162

Bibliography................................... 169

Index of Pattern Names & Makers.................. 171

Acknowledgments

The enthusiasm and support of the members of our antique club, "Tickled By Time" has been a key factor in writing this book. Not just for the contributions of glassware to photograph, but also for the encouragement and support to move forward with this project.

A special acknowledgment must go to Lyle Fokken, the co-author of this book. Without his photography and tremendous supply of unique glass items, this book would not have been possible. His remarkable knowledge of glass and research material has been phenomenal.

Acknowledgment also needs to go to Guy Allen, who shared close to 50 glass items with us to use in this book, and who's technological skills were invaluable.

For everyone, including our local bookstore, who has shown a special interest in focusing this book on the memorable colored glassware, we express our deepest gratitude.

Reflections

The chapter on Reflections in the first book I wrote, in 1998, has a direct impact on this book in relation to the current economic situation. In the chapter I reflected from my own experience on the turbulent times of the Depression era. During the 1920s and 1930s, American families struggled and found it hard to imagine that economics would ever get better. Morale and hopes were low, so in response, glass manufacturers began producing bright and cheery colors to bring a ray of sunshine into American homes. Today, the economy is facing some of the same hardships that were experienced during the Depression. Still, bright colored glass can bring a ray of sunshine into our homes, by our collecting, displaying, and using the wonderful glass of our past.

Introduction

Due to the tremendous response of my previous books published on Depression and Elegant glassware, I've received numerous requests for a fifth book on this wonderful collectable glass.

This book focuses on 16 of the most popular and intriguing colors, and identifies over 250 different glass patterns. Each chapter gives a brief history of the color, followed by various photographs of items in that color. Years of production and a current value are given for all items.

Our chief goal is to encourage the collecting and use of vintage glass. Trends of collecting seem to be changing constantly. Years ago collectors desired every piece made in a particular pattern, but not today. Currently we've noticed that collectors seem to buy only the pieces that intrigue them, or pieces that they can use. Another trend we see quite often is collecting a particular color of glass, which we hope this book will encourage. The colors and their inherent charm continue to brighten our tables, decorating them for the seasons and special holidays.

Depression glass still captivates the generations today. Its variety of rich, deep, and vibrant colors attracts people, collectors and non-collectors alike. Those who have gathered this glassware cherish their collections and have something wonderful to pass on to their families. What a remarkable and memorable inheritance.

Price Guidelines

The prices listed in this guide are for items in mint condition—meaning no chips, cracks, flakes, or surface wear. Slight imperfections due to manufacturing may be ok, as long as they are not a distraction to the item.

Values are based on the realized selling prices in antique stores, glass shows, and on the internet. Prices, however, can vary from region to region and should be used only as a guide; they are not intended to set prices. What a collector is willing to pay ultimately sets the value.

Chapter One
Pink - The Classic Color

Pink, the soft yet brilliant eye-catching color, is always associated with Depression glass. It is one of the classic colors easily recognized by the majority of collectors and even non-collectors. It can be found in almost all of the Depression glass patterns, including many kitchenware items. When people see pink glass they often refer to it as "Grandma's glass." Pink has to be one of the most popular glass colors to collect. As soon as you get two or three pieces in a grouping, you'll be hooked to search for more.

The majority of glass manufacturers produced shades of pink, as it was a popular color in the 1920s. It was the sensation of the Pittsburgh Glass Exhibit, as well as in the homes of America during this era. Flamingo, Cheriglo, Rose, and Azalea are just a few of the names the glass companies used to market their pink glassware.

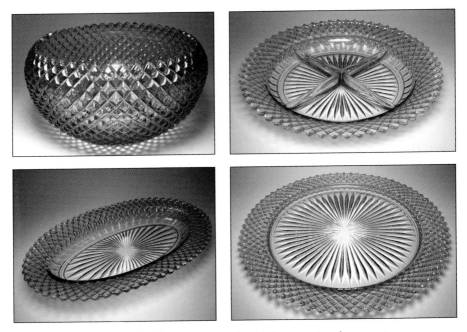

Miss America, Hocking Glass Company, 1933-1938. It is a very popular pattern, with a center star design and diamond point border. Treasured as the pattern was named to capture the essence of American patriotism. Large 8 inch bowl $115, 4-part relish $30, Dinner plate $45, Oval celery dish $45.

A very special piece of pink Depression era glass is the Miss America bowl that I inherited from my grandmother. This was one of my first pieces of old glass, and the reason for my addiction for collecting glass of the Depression era. This bowl is one of the most cherished pieces in my collection.

Old Colony, "Open Lace," Hocking Glass Company, 1935-38. An easy recognized pattern by the open loop type edges and radial star center. It is a favorite pattern among veteran collectors. 10.5" Divided relish $35, Flower bowl with crystal frog $50, 10.5" Dinner plate $40.

Cherry Blossom, Jeannette Glass Company, 1930-1939. It is a very popular pattern with an overall molded brocade of cherries and leaves on the outside. 8" Pitcher $75, 9" Grill plate $35.

Sierra, "Pinwheel," Jeannette Glass Company, 1931-1933.
This is a very art deco pattern with its pinwheel shaped design. Check
the points carefully as they are prone to chip. Water pitcher $150, 4.5"
Tumbler $80, Cup & Saucer $25.

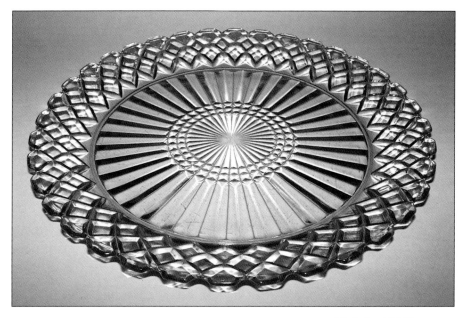

Waterford Waffle, Hocking Glass Company, 1938-1944. A late Hocking pattern made in table settings of crystal and pink. Bottoms have radial sunburst lines, with a triple concentric ring of blocks close to the center. The sides have a block or waffle design. 10" Dinner plate $25, Handled cake plate $24, 8.25" Large serving bowl $36.

Rosemary, "Dutch Rose," Federal Glass Company, 1935-1937. This pattern has a center bouquet of roses placed between overlapping looped designs that contain small roses in between. Grill plate $30.

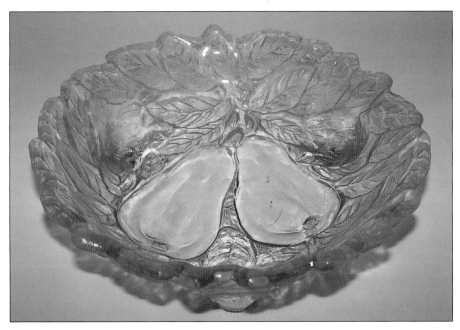

Avocado, "Sweet Pear," Indiana Glass Company, 1923-1933. This is a very attractive pattern with two pears in the center, surrounded by a leafed border. 6" Footed bowl $28.

Sharon, "Cabbage Rose," Federal Glass Company, 1935-1939. This is a very popular and attractive pattern with a center motif of small roses, which are divided by a spoke design. Butter dish w/cover $65, 10.5" Fruit bowl $50.

Diamond Quilted, Imperial Glass Company, 1920s-1930s. This is a simple pressed pattern with a lovely visual diamond optic. The centers of the plates are plain and the borders have an interlocking diamond effect. 8" Luncheon plate $10, 7" Bowl $16, Sugar $12, Creamer $12, Candlesticks (pair) $30.

Flower Garden With Butterflies, U.S. Glass Company, 1920s. Flower Garden attracts collectors like flowers attract butterflies. For collectors it is very difficult to find which keeps the prices quite high. The variety of pieces and color is numerous. Ashtray with cigarette pack and match holders $185.

Frances, Central Glass Company, 1920s-1930s. This is a wonderful pattern that is not often correctly identified. It has wide ribs emanating from the center, which have notches out of them creating a very art deco style. Footed sugar bowl $30.

Doric, Jeannette Glass Company, 1935-1938. This is a classic appearing glass pattern that has a circle of windows around the outer parts, with a stylized floral type design inside every other one. Sugar with cover $40, Creamer $20.

Tea Room, Indiana Glass Company, 1926-1931. This is an early pattern made for restaurants and soda fountains. It is a very prized art deco pattern that is seldom found in excellent condition because of all the pointed corners, which are prone to chip. 5" Footed Tumbler $45, Pitcher $185, Oval vegetable bowl $70. (*Courtesy of Guy Allen*)

Manhattan, "Horizontal Ribbed," Anchor Hocking Glass Company, 1938-1943. This art deco pattern is unlike most Anchor Hocking other patterns. It has concentric ribs or rings, which catch light, creating a stunning look. It is one of a few patterns where many collectors prefer crystal to a color. Berry bowl with handles $25, Candy dish with ball feet $20, Tumbler $25, Footed compote $60.

Dogwood, "Apple Blossom," MacBeth-Evans Glass Company, 1929-1932. A mold etched pattern with an all over floral brocade pattern. The plates have three large center blossoms and foliage as a center motif, while the outer rims contain more dogwood blossoms and leaves. 9.25" plate $40.

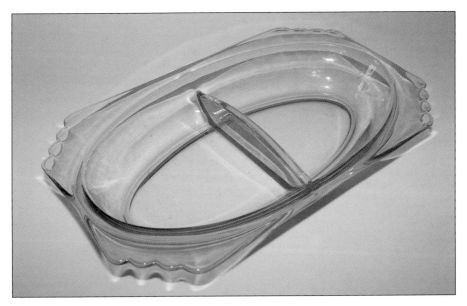

Mayfair, Fostoria Glass Company, 1931-1943. This is a plainer pattern with a square shape. The four corners each have four small scallops. Other companies had very similar patterns, but the number of corner scallops, and their shape differentiates the patterns. 8.5" Oval divided relish $20.

Mayfair, "Open Rose," Hocking Glass Company, 1931-1937. This pattern is very popular with over 50 different items made. The center has a circle of roses, followed by outward spokes and then more flowers on the outer edge. Cake plate $40, Divided relish tray $38, Water Goblet $80, Sugar $25, Creamer $25.

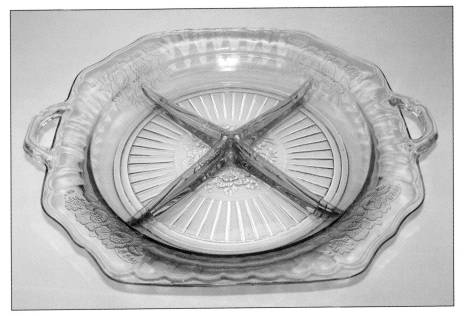

Line #323, Paden City Glass Company, Loaf cream and sugar. A two-piece set often referred to as a Domino Set because of the brand of sugar cubes that would be placed on the bottom tray. $50.

Jubilee, Lancaster Glass Company, c. 1930s. An elegant cut pattern decorated with an exquisite floral and leaf design defined by twelve petal flowers with an open center. Sugar $40, Creamer $45.

Twisted Optic, Imperial Glass Company, 1927-1930. These have a beautiful swirling pattern on underside. In recent years, it's been questioned as for certain if Imperial made these or not. Until further information surfaces, I consider them Twisted Optic. Candlesticks (pair) $22.

Adam, Jeannette Glass Company, 1932-1934. An attractive "garden like" pattern with its profusion of flowers, leaves, and fern type scrolls. Pitcher $75, 4.5" tumbler $35, 7.75" Bowl $30, 4.75" bowl $20, Candy jar with lid $135. (*Pitcher and tumbler courtesy of Marlene McCabe*)

Sunflower, Jeannette Glass Company, c. 1920s. An appealing pattern to collectors, but difficult to find pieces, except the large 10" round cake plate, which was a premium gift. A mold etched pattern with large stylized sunflowers in the center. Keep your eyes open for the rare trivet, which looks like a child's size version of the larger cake plate. Creamer $20, Sugar $22, Cake plate or stand $20.

Geneva, powder jar, New Martinsville Glass Company, c. 1930s. A fine diamond cut-like pattern with fancy flume cover finial. This was originally sold with matching perfumes, which have the same fancy stopper tops. $30. (*Courtesy of Marlene McCabe*)

Oyster & Pearl, Anchor Hocking Glass Company, 1938-1940. A short-lived pattern, but very attractive with its vertical spaced lines with pearl accents and scalloped edge. Only accessory pieces were made, but still wonderful to collect. 10.5" Deep fruit bowl $25, 13.5" Serving plate $40, Divided Relish Dish $30, Candlestick (pair) $45.

Cupid, Paden City Glass Company, c. 1930s. This is a very whimsical acid etched pattern containing two-winged cupids facing each other. Not easy to find and priced high when you do see it. Creamer $125, Sugar $125, Elliptical Vase $675.

Ardith, Paden City Glass Company, 1920s & 1930s. This is a wonderful acid etched pattern of cherry blossoms and leaves in a very attractive design. 8.25" Plate $40, Tumbler $50, Footed sherbet $35, Cup & saucer $75.

Notched Square, Liberty Works, c. 1920s. This is a very interesting pattern with uniquely styled handles. A full table service was made but little is found today. Plates are square in shape, identical to the feet on this cream and sugar. Creamer $25, Sugar $25.

Chapter Two

Green - A Vibrant
and Refreshing Color

Green is the typical Depression color featured in so many tableware settings of the 1920s and 1930s. Green can be found in many patterns and is popular with collectors. There are many variations in the shade of green from company to company. Many patterns were made, even within the same company. Companies worked very hard to keep the shade of a particular pattern being produced consistent, even over several years. Families during the depression sometimes could only afford to purchase a few pieces at a time, so keeping the color correct was important for future sales. Anchor Hocking was one of the largest producers of green glassware, including many patterns of Depression Glass and lots of kitchenware.

I grew up with a lot of green colored glassware. For me, green has a sentimental connection, as my mother's luncheon and dinner services were green. I particularly remember the pattern "Cloverleaf" that was produced by Hazel Atlas in the early 1930s. It is a very attractive pattern with a clover motif around the edge.

It seems as if so many collectors carry a torch for transparent green Depression Glass. It is delicate and somewhat like a brilliant apple green. Just like pink, it is often referred to as "Grandma's Glass."

Cloverleaf, Hazel-Atlas Glass Company, 1930-1936.
This is a mold etched pattern that has three leaf clovers going around the border and on the inside area of the plates. Green is the favored color to collect, as it fits best with the clover theme. Footed tumbler $40, Flat tumbler $60, Cup & Saucer $15, 8" Luncheon plate $10, Salt & Pepper shakers $60. (*Courtesy of Guy Allen*)

Avocado, "Sweet Pear," Indiana Glass Company, 1923-1933. This is a very attractive pattern with two pears in the center, surrounded by a leafed border. Creamer $40, Sugar $40, Cup & saucer $75. (*Courtesy of Guy Allen*)

Spiral, Hocking Glass Company, 1928-1930. This pattern is very similar to the Twisted Optic pattern, however the pinwheel design swirls to the right in Spiral. Preserve w/slot in lid for spoon $70.

Diamond Block, "Little Jewel," Imperial Glass Company, c. 1920s. An attractive pattern, which is becoming more popular today, consisting of rows of diamond blocks, a sunburst bottom, and notched edge. 8.5" Celery tray $30.

Tea Room, Indiana Glass Company, 1926-1931. This is an early pattern made for restaurants and soda fountains. It is a very prized art deco pattern that is seldom found in excellent condition because of all the pointed corners, which are prone to chip. Creamer $30, Sugar $30, Handled tray $50, Cup $75, Saucer $30. (*Courtesy of Guy Allen*)

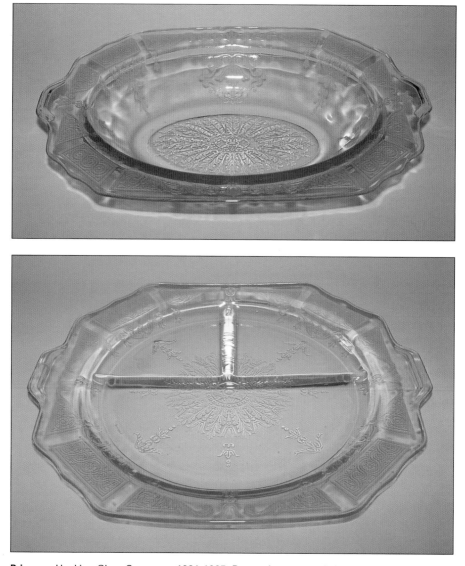

Princess, Hocking Glass Company, 1931-1935. Pattern is octagonal shaped, center motif is a snowflake with spokes, and decorated with lines flowers and leaves. Oval vegetable bowl $30, Handled grill plate $15. (*Bowl courtesy of Marlene McCabe*)

Floral and Diamond Band, U.S. Glass Company. 1927-1931. A deeply pressed floral pattern made to appear like early cut glass. Flowers and leaves wrap around the sides and a diamond pattern along the top. 8" Large berry bowl $25.

Cameo, "Ballerina," Hocking Glass Company, 1930-1934. It is an easy pattern to identify, as it is one of few patterns with a human figure as part of the design. Little dancing girls with long draped scarves appear in the border, while being surrounded by festoons and ribbons. Water Bottle without stopper $100, with stopper $215, Mayonnaise compote with spoon $65.

Georgian, "Lovebirds," Federal Glass Company, 1931-1936. A mold etched pattern with a subdued classical appearance. It is often called Lovebirds because of the pair of birds in the pattern. Sugar $20, Creamer $20, 8" Luncheon plate $15. (*Plate courtesy of Marlene McCabe*)

Egg Harbor, Liberty Works, c. late 1920s. This pattern was available in a full dinner service. It is very attractive, even though plain, with pieces cone shaped with a slightly scalloped top containing 6 points. Egg Harbor has a paneled optic in the lower bowl. Make a note that without the optic it is not part of the true Egg Harbor line. Cream & Sugar $30.

Florentine, Cambridge Glass Company, c. 1920s-1930s. An elegant acid etched band found on many Cambridge items. It is sometimes seen with gold over the etching. Shape #394 Tab handled ice tub $65.

Betty Mae, decanter set, Paden City Glass Company, c. 1920s. This is a lovely small cordial set consisting of an oblong decanter and stopper, six small shot glass sized tumblers, and a handled tray. Note that there is a ridge on the tray top to keep the decanter from slipping around. $95.

Black Forest, Paden City Glass Company, c. 1920s-1930s. This is an etched pattern, which depicts moose standing in a forest and a moose defending himself from a barking dog. Ice Bucket with metal handle $130.

Crow's Foot, Paden City Glass Company, c. 1930s. This pattern can have a square or round shape; both are considered to be Crow's Foot. The pattern has four rows of teardrops followed by a fan shaped feature that looks almost like a bird track. 10″ footed bowl $45.

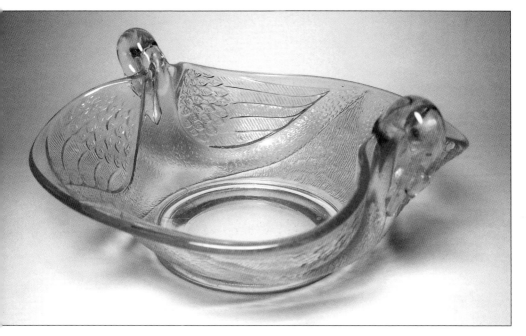

Swan Bowl, Dugan Glass Company, c. 1930s. This is an interesting bowl that has molded swan heads that form handles. It makes a wonderful centerpiece on the dinning table. $35.

Fountain Line, Jenkins Glass Company, c. 1920s-1930s. This pattern has a rippled wave like pattern that wraps around the sides. 8" Berry bowl $35. (*Courtesy of Carol Hall*)

Sunflower, Jeannette Glass Company, c. 1920s. An appealing pattern to collectors, but difficult to find pieces, except the large 10" round cake plate, which was a premium gift. A mold etched pattern with large stylized sunflowers in the center. Cake plate or stand $20, Creamer $20, Sugar $25.

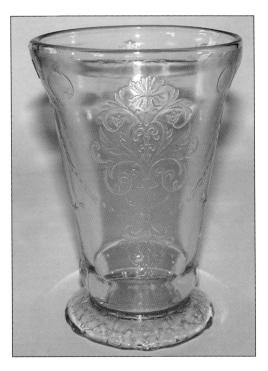

Bowknot, Maker unknown, c. 1930s. Swags of garland tied up in bows adorn this pattern. The edges and feet of most of the pieces have a slight scallop shape. 5" Tumbler $25.

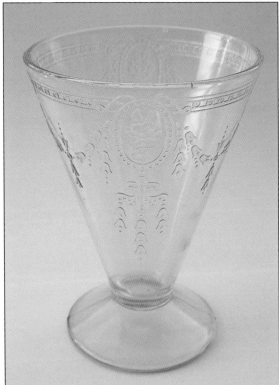

Rose Cameo, Belmont Tumbler Company, 1931. A very small pattern line, but attractive with and encircled rose with some surrounding foliage. 5" Tumbler $20.

Block Optic, Anchor Hocking Glass Company, 1929-1933. This pattern has a typical 1930s art deco style with wide concentric rings set off in blocks. It is heavy in appearance, yet light and fragile. Creamer $20, Sugar $20, Cup $9, Saucer $10.

Pebbled Rim, "Melba," L.E. Smith Glass Company, 1928-1932. This pattern is a rather plain design with only a bumpy border edge. A full dinnerware service was available. Candlesticks (pair) $40. (*Courtesy of Marlene McCabe*)

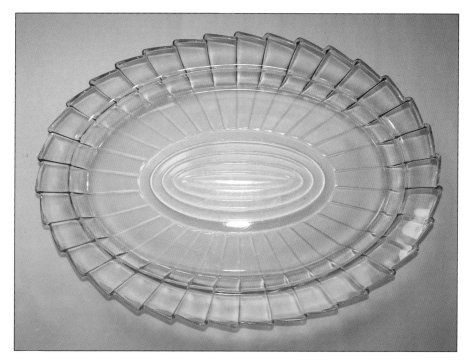

Sierra, "Pinwheel," Jeannette Glass Company, 1931-1933.
This is a very art deco pattern with its pinwheel shaped design. Check the points carefully as they are prone to chip. Oval platter $85.

Mayfair, "Open Rose," Hocking Glass Company, 1931-1937. This pattern is very popular with over 50 different items made. The center has a circle of roses, followed by outward spokes and then more flowers on the outer edge. Center handled serving tray $80. (*Courtesy of Marlene McCabe*)

Balda, Central Glass Works, c. 1920s-1930s. This is an etched pattern full of scrolling elegant flourishes, which repeats around the edges to form a border. Cheese & Cracker 2-piece set $75.

Horseshoe, "No. 612," Indiana Glass Company, 1930-1933. This pattern is entirely decorated in one uninterrupted design of an elaborate scrolling that forms a snowflake. Part of the design resembles a horseshoe, which is how it got its name. Sugar $25, Creamer $25. (*Courtesy of Marlene McCabe*)

Chapter Three
Yellow - A Golden Topaz

Yellow is a wonderful color that always makes me think of Spring dandelions. A table filled with yellow glass is quite impressive. It also compliments well with many other colors. Used as an accent with black, green, or crystal glass, it can be quite stunning as a table setting.

There are many shades of yellow glass, from a true yellow to a light amber color. Glass manufactures used many different names to describe their particular shade. Topaz, Primrose, Sahara, Canary, and Mandarin Gold are just a few of the names companies used to describe it. Some of the yellows, made by Fenton and Tiffin for example, glow a bright green color when under a black light and are sometimes referred to as Vaseline. The term Vaseline glass however has become rather generic over the years to include just about anything that glows, including many green glass pieces.

The first piece of yellow Depression Glass I purchased was a piece of the "Cameo" pattern made by Hocking Glass Company. It is one of very few glass patterns that contain a human figure in the design. I think it was the figure of the dancing girl that created the passion to hunt for more.

Lorain, "Basket," Indiana Glass Company, 1929-1932. This is an attractive pattern that has conventional baskets of flowers with a center of scrolls and garlands. The overall shape of the line is square with rounded corners. 11.5" Platter $40, Sherbet $30.

Cameo, "Ballerina," Hocking Glass Company, 1930-1934. It is an easy pattern to identify, as it is one of few patterns with a human figure as part of the design. Little dancing girls with long draped scarves appear in the border, while being surrounded by festoons and ribbons. Creamer $25, Sugar $22, Tumbler $20.

Roxana, Hazel-Atlas Glass Company, 1932. This pattern is rather scarce and very little of it is found. It is a mold-etched pattern with four pointed motifs in the center that form a cross. 6" Sherbet $10.

Console Set, Tiffin Glass Company, c. 1922-1934. Wonderful four-piece set that includes matching candlesticks, bowl, and bowl base. This is a bright color, called canary, has a satin finish. Candlesticks (pair) $95, Bowl & stand $70. (*Courtesy of Anita Tanke*)

Old Sandwich, Heisey Glass Company, 1931-1956. Rows of dimples that alternate with a blank row define this pattern style. Water pitcher w/ice lip $150. (*Courtesy of Guy Allen*)

Empress, Heisey Glass Company, 1930-1938. This pattern is rather plain with the exception of a fleur-de-lis type design on the edges. It is easily confused with the Paden City Crow's Foot pattern, however it does not have the teardrops seen on Crow's Foot. 4" Tumbler $45.

Mayfair, Fostoria Glass Company, 1931-1943. This is a plainer pattern with a square shape. The four corners each have four small scallops. Other companies had very similar patterns, but the number of corner scallops, and their shape differentiates the patterns. Cups $9 each.

Baroque, Fostoria Glass Company, 1936-1966. Baroque is a wonderful pattern that is collected by many. It has a fleur-de-lis type design towards the base of each piece. Divided relish $25, Handled nappy $20.

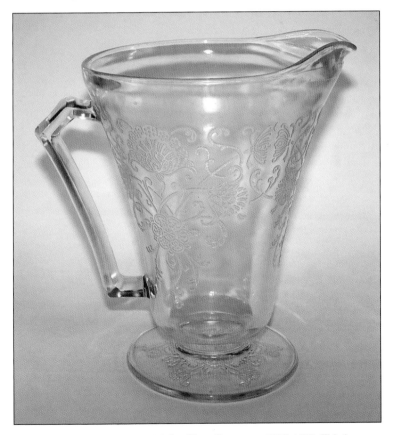

Florentine #2, "Poppy," Hazel-Atlas Glass Company, 1932-1935. This is a sister pattern to Florentine #1, which has a more scalloped edge. It has a center motif of flowers and scrolls in a pinwheel shape. Pitcher, cone footed $33.

Jubilee, Lancaster Glass Company, c. 1930s. An elegant cut pattern decorated with an exquisite floral and leaf design defined by twelve petal flowers with an open center. Sugar $20, Creamer $20, Tray $35, Cup & saucer $15.

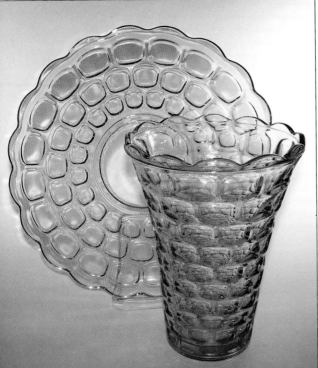

Yorktown, Federal Glass Company, c. 1950s. This pattern consists of rows or rounded corner rectangular blocks. Color is a very bright yellow. 11.5" Plate $9, Vase $15.

7-Piece beverage set, Tiffin Glass Company, c. 1930s. Lovely little center handled tray that holds 6 shot glass size cordials. Very hard to find complete. $125.

Bel-aire, Imperial Glass Company, c. 1930s. This is an etched floral pattern that appears to be either a morning glory or clematis. Dinner plate $12, Oval vegetable bowl $22.

Cable Flute, Lancaster Glass Company, c. 1932. This is a high quality vase with a ruffled top edge. There are three flaring out spines separating areas with no pattern. At the base, there is a pressed pattern containing a band of circles. $25.

Cane Landrum, "Shape #765," Lancaster Glass Company, c. 1932. A pattern that is quite detailed and uniquely designed. It has a curved up edge with points and a pressed cane pattern in the center base. $45.

Line #894, Lancaster Glass Company, c. 1930s. This is an elegant pattern with wide-open areas of glass and a center that has a pressed cane design. $28.

Cloverleaf, Hazel-Atlas Glass Company, 1930-1936.
This is a mold etched pattern that has three leaf clovers going around the border and on the inside area of the plates. Green is the favored color to collect, as it fits best with the clover theme, however yellow is much harder to find, which has driven up prices. Salt & Pepper $120, Covered candy jar $125, footed tumbler $35, Sherbet $15. (*Courtesy of Guy Allen*)

Chapter Four
Opalescent - Tones of
Opal Gemstone

Opalescent is a glass color that resembles an opal gemstone in color. Most often a translucent bluish white color mixed into the edges of a contrasting base color. The most common pattern to find in opalescent is Hobnail, which was made for many years by many different companies. The base color can be almost any color, but the opalescent edge or hobnails are almost always a white or light blue opal color.

Opalescent glass has very early beginnings in America, and seems to have a resurgence every 50 years or so. In the early 1900s Northwood, Jefferson, Hobs-Brockunier, and Phoenix were some of the major producers of opalescent glass. By the time the Depression era came along, almost all the American glasshouses produced some type of opalescent glass. Today, Fenton is the company most people identify with this glass, as they have had the longest production run of any American company.

Lattice Medallion, Northwood Glass Company, c. 1908. This is a beautiful green opalescent three-footed bowl with a double crimped edge. As the name suggests, there is a medallion and a lattice in the pressed design. $45.

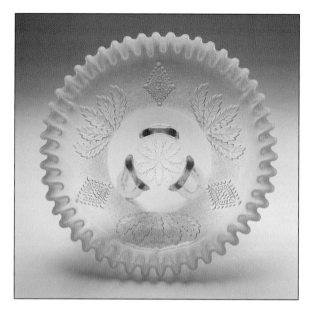

I have seen some sellers refer to opalescent glass as "Opaline" or "Pearlescent" glassware. However "Opaline" typically refers to an item with an opal translucency but is all one color, and "Pearlescent" is thought more as an iridescent exterior decoration of the surface, such as seen on Carnival glass.

Leaf and Diamond, Jefferson Glass Company, c. 1901-1907. Here is a very attractive early piece of opalescent glass. There is a stippled diamond shape and leaves in the pattern. A unique feature is the tall legs, which I surmise were easily damaged and the reason this pattern is so hard to find. $130.

Regal, Northwood Glass Company, c. 1905.
Covered butter dish in a green opalescent color.
Pattern contains blocks and panels and a simulated
cut star pattern in the base. $175.

Many Loops, Jefferson Glass Company, c. 1901-1907. This shallow bowl or card receiver is
basically a plate with three turned up edges. The pattern consists of intertwining loops with a
chevron border above and below it. $65. (*Courtesy of Marlene McCabe*)

I was fascinated by the unique color in the first bowl I found in green. It was a three-footed bowl with a pleated rim and a floral design. My second find was a blue footed bowl made by Northwood, in the Blossoms and Palms pattern, which I show later in this chapter. I have a particular fondness for opalescent bowls and never pass them up at our local auction house.

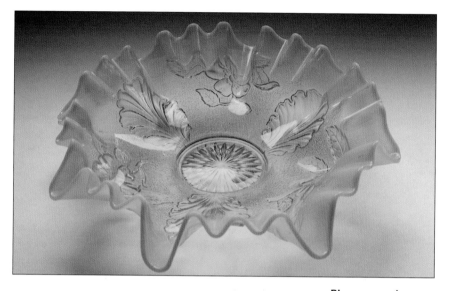

Blossoms and Palms, Northwood Glass Company, c. 1905. Here is a lovely blue opalescent card receiver with a double crimped edge. There are wild roses and palms in the pattern. $65.

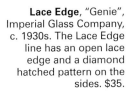

Heirloom, Fostoria Glass Company, 1959-1970. This is a 6" ribbed bon-bon with one turned up side, uniquely shaped in blue opalescent. $30.

Lace Edge, "Genie", Imperial Glass Company, c. 1930s. The Lace Edge line has an open lace edge and a diamond hatched pattern on the sides. $35.

Hobnail Opalescent, Fenton Art Glass Company, 1939-present. This company has produced many items with a hobnail design. Colors made were called French, Blue, Topaz, and Cranberry; French being the lower value and Cranberry being the highest. Blue individual cream & sugar $35, French cornucopia vase/candlestick $30, Blue mini cornucopia vase/candlestick $25, French cone vase $25, French individual cream & sugar $25, French covered mustard jar $25.

Moonstone, Anchor Hocking Glass Company, 1941-1946.
This is a hobnail pattern that is very similar to Fenton's Hobnail, however the Moonstone hobs are much more flattened and smooth. The bottoms of many of the Moonstone also have a star type pattern, which Fenton's doesn't. 6.5" handled bowl $12, Divided relish $12, Cloverleaf candy $15, Goblet $20, Luncheon plate $18, Sherbet $10, Cigarette box $30, Covered candy $30, Puff box $30.

Basket Weave with Open Edge, Fenton Art Glass Company, c. 1930s. This pattern is easy to identify by the woven basket type design on the bottoms. It is an early Fenton shape, first used to make carnival glass. 5.75" Flat bon-bon $45, Double crimped bowl $55.

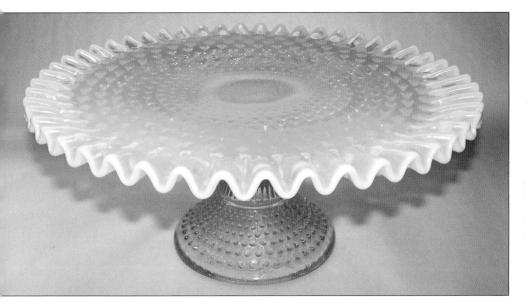

Hobnail Opalescent, Fenton Art Glass Company, 1939-present. This company has produced many items with a hobnail design. Colors made were called French, Blue, Topaz, and Cranberry; French being the lower value and Cranberry being the highest. Footed blue cake salver $110.

Canterbury, Duncan & Miller, 1938-1955. These vases are a blue opalescent with crimped tops. They have a 6 lobed bottom and are quite heavy. 8.5" Vase $125, 5" Vase $65, 3.5" Vase $35. (*Courtesy of Guy Allen*)

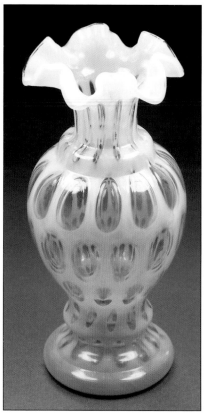

Coin Dot, Fenton Art Glass Company, 1947-1950. Here is a beautiful light blue opalescent vase with clear windows. It is blown glass with a double crimped top edge. $195. (*Courtesy of Marlene McCabe*)

Beaded Block, Imperial Glass Company, c. 1920s and 1930s. A popular pattern of square panels separated by vertical and horizontal beaded lines. "6 Vase $55. (*Courtesy of Marlene McCabe)*

Coral, Jefferson Glass Company, c. 1901-1907. This dish is Vaseline yellow with an open edge border and scrolling worm like pattern. $65.

Ruffles and Rings, Northwood Glass Company, c. 1905-1910. These are a white opalescent with a pattern containing interlocking rings and a leaf like design by the legs. This is a pattern first made by Jefferson Glass Company. Fine crimped bowl $50, Larger crimp bowl $45.

Pump and Trough, Northwood Glass Company, c. 1905-1910. This is a very whimsical cream and sugar set shaped like a pump made from a wooden log. Beware of reproductions, having a flat edge on the pump top. $125. *(Courtesy of Guy Allen)*

Jolly Bear, Jefferson Glass Company, c. 1901-1907. A dancing bear in the center identifies this pattern of opalescent glass. It is also often found with gold decoration and referred to as goofus glass. $75.

Chapter Five
Cobalt Blue - The
Mystique Color

Cobalt blue is such a deep, rich, and strong blue that it is extremely popular with everyone, not just glass collectors. For this reason, this color glass does not stay in the antique stores for very long, regardless of the pattern or rarity. Acquiring pieces can be a challenge as the popularity also keeps the prices high.

The glass manufactures during the Depression years used many names to refer to this dark cobalt color. Ritz Blue, Regal Blue, Dark Blue, and Royal Blue are just a few of the names used. Paden City Glass Company was one of the few glasshouses that actually used the term Cobalt to advertise the color.

We are all familiar with the cobalt breakfast set of a mug, pitcher, and cereal bowl featuring the white image of Shirley Temple. The set was made by Hazel Atlas and offered as a premium gift by General Mills cereal in 1936. In the offering, the color was referred to as Sapphire Blue. I remember a set owned by my neighbor years ago and still remember how I just loved the color.

Another fond memory of mine, and so many others, is the Evening in Paris perfume. This perfume was introduced in the mid-1920s and sold in cobalt blue bottles. It was extremely popular for many years and the first real grown-up scent for many young girls. I have to think that the appeal of its signature cobalt blue bottle had something to do with the perfumes popularity. As a young girl, it was always my favorite and my mother would buy it for me often. My purse always contained the long slim vial size bottle with its matching blue tassel on its cover.

Left and right:
Moderntone, Hazel-Atlas Glass Company, c. 1930s and 1940s. This is an admired pattern for its rich coloring and for its simplistic style with widely spaced concentric rings that are indicative of the 1930s art deco styles. Salad Plate $12, Sherbet $15, Shaker $20, Sugar $15, Creamer $15. (*Cream and sugar courtesy of Marlene McCabe*)

Shirley Temple pitcher, Hazel-Atlas Glass Company, c. 1936. This pitcher was given away as a premium gift by General Mills cereal. Shirley Temple, whose image appears on the pitcher, was born in 1928 and starred in numerous movies and was cherished for her dimples and curls. Beware of reproductions. $40.

Royal Lace, Hazel-Atlas Glass Company, 1934-1941. This is a fantastic console set with an overall lacey design that is very popular with collectors. Candleholders (pair) $195, Console bowl $100. (*Courtesy of Linda Wasko*)

Aurora, Hazel-Atlas Glass Company, c. late 1930s. This is a vertical paneled pattern with two bands around the top edge. There are not many items to collect in this line, but it still has been quite popular. Creamer $28, Cereal bowl $20.

Utility Bowl, Hazel-Atlas Glass Company, c. 1930s. Here is a large kitchen bowl with wide bulging vertical panels and a rolled over rim. Kitchen bowls in this wonderful cobalt blue are becoming very hard to find. $85. (*Courtesy of Anita Tanke*)

Fine Rib ball pitcher, Hazel-Atlas Glass Company, c. late 1930s. This ball shaped juice or water pitcher is has a classic art deco style to it. Fine ribs wrap around the neck and up and down the sides. Two sizes were made, this being the smaller. Matching tumblers can also be found to make a spectacular set. $45. (*Courtesy of Linda Wasko*)

Deco Fan, Central Glass Works, c. 1930s. Deco Fan is a very elaborate pattern with fancy handles and scalloped corners. It is typically found in crystal and seldom found in colors. These examples have an etched and gold encrusted design. Divided relish $75, Sugar $30, Serving bowl $65.

Crow's Foot, Paden City Glass Company, c. 1930s. This pattern can have a square or round shape; both are considered to be Crow's Foot. The pattern has four rows of teardrops followed by a fan shaped feature that looks almost like a bird track. This example has silver overlay. Handled tray $140.

Georgian, Duncan & Miller Glass Company, 1928. Many companies made patterns very similar to this but Duncan was the only company to have oval shaped cream and sugars. It's a classic honeycomb design that was popular for many years. Sugar $25, Creamer $25, Luncheon plate $8.

Moondrops, New Martinsville Glass Company, 1932-1940s. A very complete pattern of numerous unique items made in various vibrant colors. Very art deco in style with fan shaped stoppers and finals. Shot glass $20, Stemmed cordial $35, Large decanter $85, Small decanter $75.

Lincoln Inn, Fenton Art Glass Company, 1928-1937. This pattern is another that displays the art deco styles popular in the 1930s. It has fine vertical ribbing with concentric rings in the lower part of the design. Smoke set (3-peice) $49.

Fish canapé trays, Imperial Glass Company, c. 1930s. Using fish-shaped trays to hold your food at luncheons had to be great fun! Each has a ring to hold a small tumbler in place. $15.ea

Two-tone bud vase, Huntington Tumbler Company, c. 1930s. Here's a stunning vase with a crystal clear foot. It has a sleek shape with a flared and crimped top edge. The underside of the foot has concentric rings that appear to ripple when you see them from the top. $49.

El Rancho, Bryce Glass Company, 1960-1966. El Rancho is a pattern that almost appears like a crumpled up paper bag that someone tried to straighten out. It is high quality glass with a deep rich cobalt blue. Tumblers $9.ea, Plate $12, Finger bowl $5.

Chanticleer, Duncan & Miller Glass Company, c. 1920s-1930s. This rooster pattern was quite popular in barware lines but not very much of it is found. The tumblers have very stylized roosters around their bases. $75.

Glades, Paden City Glass Company, c. 1930s. This pattern is art deco with vertical ribs on the sides. This unique cigarette box has a built in ashtray that serves as a cover. $90.

Chapter Six

Amber - A Golden Brown Color

Amber, a yellowish brown with sometimes an orange tint, was made in many shades and was popular during the Depression years. Amber glass first came into favor in America just after the Civil War, and can be found in many early pressed glass patterns. Popularity slowed, but again amber had a resurgence when the very fine glasshouses of the early 1920s who previously were making mostly blown crystal, moved into the Golden Age of Colored Glass. Large amounts of amber glass were being sold so the Depression Glass Manufacturers quickly followed with many less expensive pressed patterns and shades for the general public. The popularity of collecting amber Depression Glass seems to fluctuate every decade or so. Currently I've noticed an increased interest so don't pass up any pieces you find attractive.

I purchased my first piece of amber glass in the 1980s, a candy jar in the Diana pattern by Federal Glass Company. At the time of the purchase I was not very enthused by the color, as it seemed no one else liked it. But when I got it home and really looked at it, I began to fall in love with the swirling pattern and golden amber glow. Today, I bring out all my amber colored glass in the autumn to decorate and use during the fall season. Guests always seem to love it as much as I do!

Diana, Federal Glass Company, 1937-1941. A simple pattern of fine swirled lines leading out from the center with wide rims of slightly larger curved lines. Covered Candy $40.

Rosemary, "Dutch Rose," Federal Glass Company, 1935-1937. This pattern has a center bouquet of roses placed between overlapping looped designs that contain small roses in between. Cup $8, Saucer $5, Sugar $15, Creamer $15, Oval platter $18. (*Courtesy of Marlene McCabe*)

Normandy, "Bouquet & Lace," Federal Glass Company, 1933-1940. This pattern has a motif of lattice and floral in the design. Creamer $20, Sugar $10.

Patrician, Federal Glass Company, 1933-1937. Pattern is pressed; plates have an irregular edge with a scalloped inner border. Center motif is round with an eight-spoke design surrounded by a scrolled ten-point star. 11" Dinner plate $25.

Sharon, "Cabbage Rose," Federal Glass Company, 1935-1939. Here is a very popular and attractive pattern with a center motif of a curved spray of roses. More roses and spokes divide the sides. 8.5 Large berry bowl $9. *(Courtesy of Robyn Tanke)*

Glass utility bowl, Federal Glass Company, c. 1930s. This is a very useful kitchen utility bowl with fine ribbing on the underside. $15. *(Courtesy of Anita Tanke)*

Madrid, Federal Glass Company, 1932-1939. Madrid is a very lacy overall pattern with square shapes. 5.5" Tumbler $20, 4" Tumbler $15, Luncheon plate $9, Sherbet plate $5, Cream soup bowl $15, Cup & saucer $10.

Lace Edge, "Katy," Imperial Glass Company, c. 1930s. The Katy line has an open lace edge and a diamond hatched pattern on the sides. It was made for many years and in many colors. 9" bowl $20. *(Courtesy of Sandy Goetzman)*

Orchid, Paden City Glass Company, c. 1930s. Orchid is an acid etched pattern that features orchids. Many unique items were produced including this elliptical pillow shaped vase in a metal ormolu holder. $250-$300.

Radiance, New Martinsville Glass Company, 1936-1939. This pattern has dotted rays of various lengths emanating from its base. Creamer $15, Sugar $15.

Daisy, Indiana Glass Company, 1933-1940 (amber). An attractive pattern surrounded by numerous daises and scrolls. Relish dish $24.

Sandwich, Indiana Glass Company for Tiara Exclusives, 1970-1998. This is a very attractive and useful egg plate with a sunflower and scroll design. It was made using the old mold from the Duncan & Miller Sandwich line. The old will have a ground and polished bottom, the newer versions will not. $25.

Chapter Seven
Amethyst - A Rich Purple Color

Amethyst is a strong purple color named after the gemstone of the same name. It is a color that you do not find in many Depression Era patterns, and even fewer kitchenware items. While the color had great success earlier with fine Elegant Glass, it did not catch on at first with Depression Glass. While most of the glasshouses made the color sporadically through the 1920s and 30s, most of the production was in the very late 1930s and early 1940s.

In the 1960s, Hazel Ware produced large quantities of their Moroccan Amethyst in various patterns. Collectors of these later patterns also created interest in the older amethyst. This caused a great deal of amethyst glass to disappear into collections.

There is a darker amethyst that many refer to as black amethyst. Black amethyst is glass that appears to be black, but when held to a strong light, an amethyst or purple color is visible. This color is addressed in the next chapter.

Decanter set, Fostoria Glass Company, 1934-1937. This is an interesting decanter set with and overall crinkled surface and molded dimples. $230.

My first exciting piece of amethyst glass was found on a trip to visit my sister and family in Ohio. While there, we took a drive into Kentucky, stopping at various antique malls and shops filled with wonderful glass items. It was at one of these stores that I saw a large footed bowl with a lightly crimped top sitting on a table. It attracted me so much that I darted across the room to pick it up, completely oblivious to everything else in the store. It was a "Must Have," and I love and cherish it still today. Partly because of the beauty of the glass itself and partly because of the wonderful memories it gave me.

El Rancho, Bryce Glass Company, 1955-1966. El Rancho is a pattern that almost appears like a crumpled up paper bag that someone tried to straighten out. It is high quality glass with a deep rich color. This cracker jar was called a Turnabout because the cover could be flipped over to become a stand for serving the goodies stored inside. $45. *(Courtesy of Guy Allen)*

Moroccan Amethyst, Hazel Ware - division of Continental Can, c. 1960s. This pattern has the distinct swirls and unique modern shape. There are many different patterns included under the name Moroccan, which is more of a reference to the color than the shape. Candy dish tall $35, Candy dish short $30.

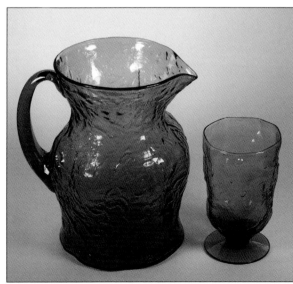

Crinkle, Morgantown Glass Company, 1940s –1960s. An abstract pattern with a smooth, but rough appearance. Many items were made in a rainbow of colors. "Ockner" shaped water jug $55, Footed tumbler $12. *(Courtesy of Guy Allen)*

Moroccan Amethyst, Hazel Ware - division of Continental Can, c. 1960s. This pattern has the distinct modern shape with square like bases. There are many different patterns included under the name Moroccan, which is more of a reference to the color than the shape. Chip & Dip set complete with wire holder $40.

No. 581 candleholders, Anchor Hocking Glass Company, c. 1950s. This is a very clever holder that can be flipped over to reveal a smaller candle socket. Funnel shaped to fit perfectly with the 1950s modern style. $15. (pair)

Princess, Viking Glass Company, c. 1952-1960s. The Princess line is known by the rippled pattern on the undersides of the bowls and plates. This is a footed vase called a Flowerlite, which should have a crystal flower frog insert on the top. $65. (Complete w/frog) *(Courtesy of Donna Hodson-Haag)*

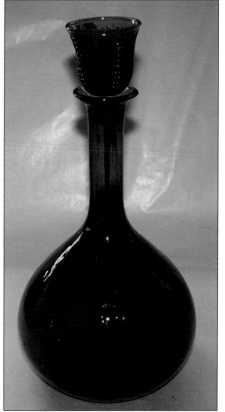

Tulip, Dell Glass Company, c. 1930s-1940s. This decanter is a hard item to find. The tulip flower pattern is only on the stopper so you can at times find the bottle miss-identified. The bottle has a dimple optic that you can see when you hold it to light. Decanter stopper only $25, Decanter complete w/stopper $450.

Ice buckets, Fostoria Glass Company, 1927-1928. These ice buckets are a light amethyst called Orchid by Fostoria. While the shapes were made for a few years, they were only made in this color for a couple. On the left is an acid etched grape brocade pattern, and on the right is a spiral optic pattern. Grape version $135, Spiral version $55. *(Courtesy of Guy Allen)*

Spartan, Fostoria Glass Company, 1927-1929. These elegant stems are from Fostoria's #5097 line and have a light amethyst bowl with crystal feet. It is the needle etching that is called Spartan. The parfait is shown without the etching. Water Goblet $20, High Sherbet $18, Parfait w/o etching $23. *(Courtesy of Guy Allen)*

Vases, Central Glass Works, c. 1919-1920s. Here are a couple of vases that are extremely hard to find in this color, as only a few were made. The tall cigar shaped vase has the gold encrusted Harding pattern. Harding was named after President Harding, who used the pattern in the White House. It contains a pair of dragons facing each other. The fan vase is acid etched with a Spanish Galleon, which is also decorated with black and gold encrusting. Harding bud vase $175-$225, Fan Vase $85-$125.

Balda, Central Glass Works, c. 1920s-1930s. This is an etched pattern full of scrolling elegant flourishes, which repeats around the edges to form a border. Pitcher $275-$350.

Catalonian, Consolidated Lamp and Glass Company, 1927-1939. This is a fantastic and unappreciated line with lots of artistic appeal. Made to look like Old Spanish glass, you will find many swirls and bubbles purposely in the glass. These examples are technically clear glass, but they have an amethyst stain over the entire exterior, so felt they fit in this chapter. Pitcher $95, Cone tumbler $15, Fan vase $35.

Chapter Eight
Black - A Dark Ebony

Black is a very early glass color, which has been called Black Milk Glass, Onyx, Ebony, Nubian Black, and other names by American manufacturers. True black glass is opaque in color and appears black throughout. Black Amethyst glass refers to glass that appears black in normal light, but shows an amethyst or purple color when held to light. I've combined both of these blacks into this same chapter, because they are very closely related.

To make black glass the workers would add manganese, a purple chemical element. The more manganese added to a batch of molten glass the darker or blacker the glass would become. To reduce expenses during the Depression years less manganese was used, creating that black amethyst effect. Other leftover glass batches of various colors could be recycled into the black batch making black glass one of the easiest and most profitable colors to make.

Ovide, Hazel Atlas Glass Company. 1930-1950s. A luncheon set was given at gas stations for buying gasoline. The set included plates, cups, saucers, bowls, creamer, and sugar. Cup $8, Saucer $4.

Westmoreland Glass Company is sometimes credited as being the first major manufacturer of black glass, but by late 1916 the popularity exploded and most glasshouses were making it in large quantities. The demand grew stronger year after year and production continuously increased. By the time of the Depression, full dinnerware sets, kitchenware, barware, and countless novelties were being made. In the 1931 Butler Brothers catalog the headline read, "Sell Ebony Black Glassware, it's all the Rage."

My favorite luncheon set is the black Ovide pattern made by the Hazel Atlas Company. My father purchased the set years ago as a premium for buying gasoline. It is a 14-piece set that I love to use on an orange tablecloth at Halloween. Would you believe the set originally sold for only $2.00?

Wide Rib, Fenton Art Glass Company, c. 1920s-1930s. A pattern with wide bulging concentric rings in a cone shape. Creamer $15, Sugar $15.

Fan Vase, Central Glass Works, c. 1920s-1930s. This is an etched pattern of thistles with gold decoration. The gold against the black is fantastic! $125.

No.2002 serving bowl, Central Glass Works, c. 1920s-1930s. This is an etched pattern with a horse and carriage that is covered in gold. The bowl is oval in shape and was originally sold with a matching serving plate. The decoration was done by the Wheeling Decorating Company. $75.

Peacock & Wild Rose, Paden City Glass Company, c. 1920s-1930s. This is another of Paden's famous bird etched patterns, and one of the easiest to find. The candle is a mushroom shape with the etching into the surface. $75.

Ardith, Paden City Glass Company, 1920s & 1930s. This is a wonderful acid etched pattern of cherry blossoms and leaves in a very attractive design. 8.25" Plate $40, Creamer $45, Sugar $45, Cup & saucer $75.

Cupid, Fostoria Glass Company, 1927-1928. Cupid is an etched brocade pattern in which the entire surface is etched with frolicking children, some building a fire. This pattern was only made for about a year so it is scarce. 11" Console bowl $250, Candlesticks (pair) $125.

Oakleaf, Fostoria Glass Company, 1928-1930. Oakleaf is an etched brocade pattern in which the entire surface is etched with oak leaves and acorns. Candy with cover $175, Cigarette box with cover $120.

Candy dish, Fostoria Glass Company, 1933-1934. This covered candy is unique as the handles are low on the side. It's a nice size and holds lots of candy. $45.

Cloverleaf, Hazel-Atlas Glass Company, 1930-1936.
This is a mold etched pattern that has three leaf clovers going around the border and on the inside area of the plates. Sugar $25, Creamer $25. *(Courtesy of Guy Allen)*

Mt. Pleasant, L. E. Smith Glass Company, 1920-1934. This is a pattern typically with scalloped edges, but other shapes made by L. E. Smith are grouped into the Mt. Pleasant line. Handled muffin plate $18, 3-footed bowl $28.

Flower Garden with Butterflies, U. S. Glass Company, c. late 1920s. A very decorative pattern profusely covered with flowers and a butterfly here and there. $250.

Candlewick, Imperial Glass Company, c. 1937. Black Candlewick was made only for a short time and typically only as a special order. It is very hard to find and expensive when you do see it. Seems everyone recognizes this pattern with its beaded edge. $275.

Vases, Louie Glass Company, c. 1930s. Here is a pair, both in a dark amethyst with crimped tops. The smaller is 5" tall and is company shape #56. The larger version is 9.5" tall and can also be found with handles. Small $12, Large $40. *(Courtesy of Donna Hodson-Haag)*

Modernistic, New Martinsville Glass Company, c. 1927-1930s. A covered candy dish in a triangular shape. The shape and stepped base are very art deco and unique. Check for damage closely as the corners are prone to chip. $125.

Flower bowl, Beaumont Tumbler Company, c. 1920s-1930s. This is a cute and useful product to hold flowers. It has three legs with a tree bark type molding. Note: The correct flower frog insert is also black glass, flatter in shape, and without the center candle socket. As shown $35, with correct flower frog $65.

Jumbo ashtray, L.E. Smith Glass Company, c. 1930s. This interesting ashtray has an elephant for a handle. It was first made by Greensburg Glass Works, which was purchased by L.E. Smith. $18.

Bel-aire, Imperial Glass Company, c. 1930s. Bel-aire is name of the etched floral pattern that appears to be either a morning glory or clematis. This center handled server is 8 sided. $35.

Charade, Diamond Glass Company, c. 1930s. This center-handled server has an open handle and practical function. It is from the #99 line made by Diamond and was dubbed as Charade by glass researcher Hazel Weatherman. Square in shape with scallops on the corners. A full table service was made. $35.

Chapter Nine
Teal - A Dark Blue Green

Teal is a color that can appear blue or green depending on the lighting and angle that it's viewed. As a color, teal is really a dark green with lots of blue in it. Glass items in this color are very appealing, but quantities are limited. In the late 1930s, Jeanette Glass Company was the largest manufacturer of the color, making full table lines and many kitchenware items. Marketed under the name Ultra-Marine, patterns like Jenny Ware, Doric and Pansy, and Swirl, were quite popular and unlike any other color being made at the time. Teal colored glass was made by other companies too and often referred to as Stiegel Green.

After finding a large sandwich plate in the Swirl pattern at an antique show years ago, I became intrigued with this color. I've purchased many other pieces of the pattern since and love serving lunch using them. Teal, intermixed with white milk glass, is quite stunning! The Swirl console bowl with its matching candleholders makes a great centerpiece.

Plymouth, Fenton Art Glass Company, 1933-1937. This pattern is quite masculine with its large round dots inside square blocks. A full line of barware was made in transparent and opalescent colors. Water Goblet $15 ea.

Swirl, "Petal Swirl," Jeanette Glass Company, 1937-1938. Swirl is a pattern that has concentric rings in the centers of most of the items, then a twisted wavy pattern on the edges. 12.5" Serving Plate $35, Sugar $18, Creamer $15.

Honey Bee candy box, Indiana Glass Company for Tiara Exclusives, 1970-1998. This is a very attractive and detailed pattern containing bees on the cover and beehives on the base. This is an old pattern that has been reissued. Older versions have short legs on the corners. This newer box in black glass is currently selling extremely well, and I expect other colors to follow in time. $30. *(Courtesy of Barb Dalton)*

Kirby, Morgantown Glass Company,
c. 1960s. These footed cocktail stems have a Stiegel Green bowl and stem with a crystal foot. They are very good quality hand blown glassware so you will not find any mold lines. $12 ea.

New Bound, Imperial Glass Company,
c. 1930s. This lovely bowl has wide swirling ribs and a gentle outward flair. It was sold as part of a console set with matching candlesticks. $45. *(Courtesy of Linda Wasko)*

Golf Ball, Morgantown Glass Company, 1931-1939. This line contains mostly stemware, but you can also find a variety of vase shapes and candy dishes. The stems and feet are crystal while the bowls are Stiegel Green. The stem shape resembles a golf ball hence its name. $20 ea.

Schaeffer, Imperial Glass Company, c.1920s-1930s. The Shaffer pattern contained a full line of barware including a cocktail shaker and decanters. The tops have a rounded shape and the bases stand on a ringed pedestal. Other companies made similar shapes so you really need to look close to identify correctly. $9 ea.

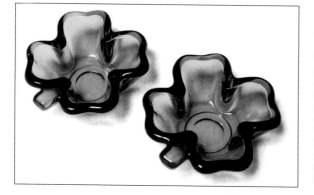

Shamrock nut bowls, Indiana Glass Company, for Colony (A division of Pitman-Dreitzer), c. 1950s. These clover shaped bowls are part of a 5-piece nut set. Included were a large 5" master nut bowl, and 4 smaller 3.5" individual bowls, all in the same clover shape. The design was patented by Pitman-Dreitzer in 1943, so production may have been slightly earlier than the 1950s. $12 ea.

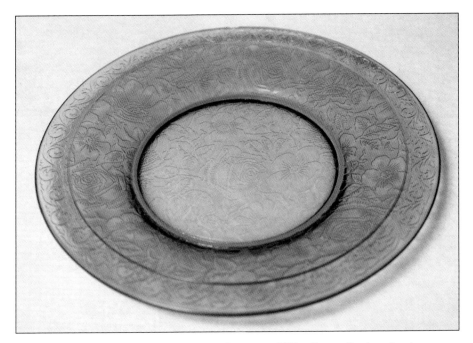

Flower Garden With Butterflies, U.S. Glass Company, 1920s. Flower Garden attracts collectors like flowers attract butterflies. For collectors it is very difficult to find which keeps the prices quite high. The variety of pieces and color is numerous. 7" Plate $18.

Golf Ball, Morgantown Glass Company, 1931-1939. This line contains mostly stemware, but you can also find a variety of vase shapes and candy dishes. The stem and foot is crystal while the bowl is Stiegel Green. The stem shape resembles a golf ball hence its name. Kimball shape ivy vase $55.

Chapter Ten
Iridescent - A Lustrous Rainbow

Iridescent is a fantastic color that can display the colors of a rainbow depending on the angle and lighting in which it is viewed. This is not so much a true color of glass, but rather a chemical treatment on the surface of the glass. The iridescent sheen is produced by applying metallic salts or oxides while the glass is still hot outside of the mold. It was a way that manufactures could mass-produce an art glass type product that was affordable to the general public.

The word Iridescent originates from Iris, the Goddess of the Rainbow in Greek Mythology. Iridescent then, is such an appropriate term to describe this type of glass.

Early iridescent glass in America was called Carnival Glass and its main production took place from 1900 to 1930. It fell out of favor for about 20 years, but in the 1950s people began to notice it again and to collect the early Carnival Glass, thus creating public demand for more iridescent glass. Manufacturers quickly moved to fill that demand and began to offer iridescent finishes on many of the crystal patterns they already had in production. This chapter contains some of the early Carnival Glass and later examples.

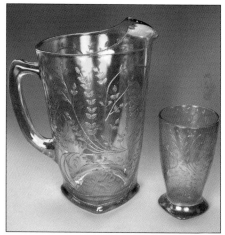

I remember finding my first piece of iridescent glass. In my usual rounds of attending garage sales, I arrived at a sale that featured mainly clothing. As I quickly scanned over the many piles of clothes, and was about to walk away, my eyes noticed a glimmer of gold. To my surprise, it was a gold iridescent covered candy dish, pattern unknown to me, but so perfect I just had to have it for the 50 cents asking price. It was this Floragold Louisa candy dish that planted the seed to eventually collect an entire set of this fantastic iridescent pattern.

Floragold, "Louisa," Jeanette Glass Company, c. 1950s. This is a pattern of branches and leaves interlocking with flowers. It is very attractive with an overall brocade design. Covered candy or cheese dish $60, Pitcher $55, Tumbler $20, Sugar $15, Creamer $15, Candlesticks $60.

Ring, "Banded Ring," Hocking Glass Company, c. 1950s. Ring is a popular pattern with horizontal ribbed bands. The line was originally made in the 1920s and 1930s, but some pieces were put back into production in the 1950s and given this iridescent finish. $20.

Iris, "Iris and Herringbone," Jeanette Glass Company, c. 1950s. Iris has always been a popular pattern with iris flowers on a herringbone background. The line was originally made in the 1920s and 1930s, but most of the gold iridescent pieces were made in the 1940s and 1950s. Pitcher $60, Sherbet $14, Tumbler $20, Tall vase $30.

Normandy, "Bouquet & Lace," Federal Glass Company, 1933-1940. This pattern has a motif of lattice and floral in the design. Sunburst was the name Federal used to refer to their gold iridescent finish. 11" Grill plate $8, Sherbet $7.

Camellia, Jeannette Glass Company, 1947-1951. This line is rather plain except for the bottom, which has a large pressed flower pattern. Even the punch cups have the flower bottom. 7 piece eggnog set $35. *(Courtesy of Guy Allen)*

Palm Leaf, Fostoria Glass Company, 1929. Made for only one year this etched and iridescent pattern is beyond elegant. It has a brocade pattern of palms leaves on a stylized art deco background. Mother of Pearl is the name Fostoria used to refer to their iridescent finishes. Oval covered candy $275, whipped cream pail w/metal handle $400-$450, Tall covered urn $450-$550.

Swirl, Northwood Glass Company, c. 1905-1910. These tumblers are rather plain on the outside, but inside the have a molded spiral pattern. The insides are marked with the Northwood "N" inside a circle. The gold finish over clear glass is deep and rich. $18 ea.

American Beauty Rose, Imperial Glass Company, c. 1913-1980s. This early piece of carnival glass has a gold iridescence on crystal glass. It is deeply pressed with a rose pattern. Imperial also called this line American Beauties, collectors and many books call it Lustre Rose. It was made for many years in various colors and finishes. Footed fern dish $70. *(Courtesy of Anita Tanke)*

Holly, "Holly and Berries," Fenton Art Glass Company, c. 1911. This is a simple but elegant pattern of leaves and berries reaching out from the center of the plate. This is crystal glass with a gold iridescence. $175. *(Courtesy of Marlene McCabe)*

Windmill, "Double Dutch," Imperial Glass Company, c. 1912. This ruffled edge bowl has a pressed glass pattern inside that features a Dutch scene including a windmill in the center. The glass is a green Imperial called Helios. Imperial reissued some pieces again in the 1960s. $45. *(Courtesy of Anita Tanke)*

Circled Scroll, Dugan Glass Company, c. 1910. A vase with an interesting beginning molded as a tumbler, but pulled up into a vase form while the glass was still pliable. The glass itself is purple with circular pressed pattern. $180.

Diamond Rib & Rustic vases, Fenton Art Glass Company, c. 1911. On the left is the Diamond Rib pattern and on the right is the Rustic pattern. Both have tall pulled up sides distorting the molded designs. The tops are hand shaped and formed in such a way to make something plain into something truly elegant. Left $40, Right $55. *(Courtesy of Jolene Tanke)*

Yorktown, Federal Glass Company,
c. 1950s. Yorktown has oval thumbprint type impressions around the outside that get larger as they get to the edges of the plates or tops of the tumblers. It is clear glass with a very light iridescence. 4" Juice tumbler $6 ea.

Fire-King Peach Lustre, Anchor Hocking Glass Corporation, c. 1950s. These handled glass dishes are great for warming food. They have a horizontal ribbed pattern and a gold iridescence on white glass. $8 ea.

Chapter Eleven
Jadite - The Opaque Green

This opaque green jade color glass is quite unique and very popular with kitchenware collectors. The McKee Glass Company first produced it in significant amounts in the early 1930s. Growing sales of this opaque color caused other manufacturers to quickly join in with their production of the color. Jeanette Glass Company was the first to use the name Jadite in its advertising. Over the years, Jadite, or Jadeite, has become a generic name to describe this color of glass, regardless of who made it. Anchor Hocking is likely the most recognized manufacturer due to its Fire-King lines of the 1940s. Many of these lines were produced for several years, even into the 1970s.

When you think of Jadite, you tend to first think about all the kitchenware items made. Spice sets, canister sets, and graduated mixing bowls have always been popular to assemble. But don't forget about the full dinnerware lines, which were also made by many companies. Many of these are referred to as clambroth, a slightly more translucent Jadite, but still a nice compliment to your collection.

Jeanette Glass Company, c. 1930s-1940s. This range set is part of a full array of items with the inverted lower rib pattern. So popular that the line is currently being reproduced. A new or missing cover should raise red flags that you may have found a new item. Salt $40, Pepper $40, Dripping jar (missing lid) $95. *(Courtesy of Guy Allen)*

I particularly love the Jadite and Black glass combination and find it very attractive. Jadite cups on black saucers are wonderful at fall get-togethers. It's wonderful to collect old glass, but even better when you can use it!

Fire-King batter pitcher, Anchor Hocking Glass Corporation, c. 1940s-1950s. This is a very functional kitchen item for mixing and then pouring liquids. There is a version with a wide top band, and another with a narrower one. The wider 1" version is typically priced about 20% more than the narrower one. $40. *(Courtesy of Guy Allen)*

Fire-King Restaurant Ware, Anchor Hocking Corporation, 1948-1967. This is a plain Jadeite pattern that is heavy and very durable. It is still popular to use as much today as it was back when it was made. If collecting for display, stay away from pieces with heavy use as they have very little value. Small bowl $25, 9" Dinner plate $25, Cup & Saucer $15. *(Courtesy of Guy Allen)*

Fire-King Restaurant Ware, Anchor Hocking Corporation, 1948-1967. This is a grouping to show various cup shapes that were made. The chocolate mug on the far right is the hardest of the 4 shapes to find. 3 Cups on the left $10-$15 ea, Far right chocolate $25-$30. *(Courtesy of Guy Allen)*

Fire-King mixing bowls, Anchor Hocking Corporation, c. 1940s-1950s. These are useful and practical and were used in almost every home at the time. There were many styles made by various makers and collectors pay a premium if they find a certain size they need to complete their nested set. Very large bowls command huge prices. Mixing Bowls shown $25-$45 depending on size. *(Courtesy of Guy Allen)*

Jane Ray, Anchor Hocking Glass Corporation, 1945-1963. Jane Ray is a thinner jade-ite dinnerware line that has always been popular with collectors. It has a fine vertical ribbing on the sides, plates being plain in the center. Covered Sugar $25, Creamer $10.

Fire-King Shell, "Regency Shell," Anchor Hocking Glass Corporation, 1965-1976. The edges of this design have a swirled pattern with a scalloped outside edge. It is often confused with the Fire-King Swirl pattern, which has a totally smooth edge verses the Shell scalloped edge. 10" Dinner plate $25 ea.

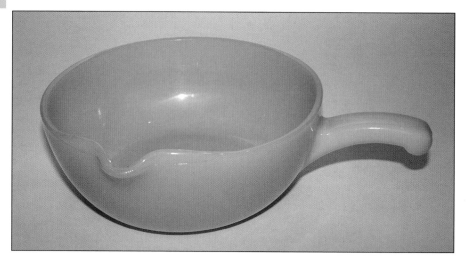

Fire-King skillet, Anchor Hocking Glass Corporation. This handled skillet was a promotional item for Gold Metal Flour. There is a two-spout version also, which is harder to find. $90. *(Courtesy of Guy Allen)*

Finger bowl & under plate, Steuben Glass Works, c. 1920s.
This lovely set is high quality glass and part of a full table service. Steuben called this color Jade Green, the foot being Alabaster. Both pieces are marked with an acid-etched, Steuben, fleur-de-lis logo on the undersides. $95.

Sunkist reamer, McKee Glass Company, c. 1940s. Every home had a reamer of some kind. Once refrigerators became commonplace in American homes, the fruit growers began to heavily market their fresh fruit. This reamer has the name Sunkist on the side. $45. *(Courtesy of Guy Allen)*

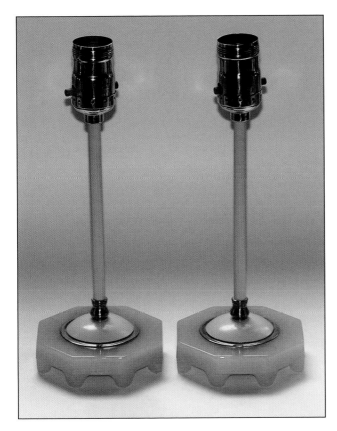

Lamps, Houzex Glass Company, c. 1920s-1930s. Many lamps were made using glass parts made of jade colored glass. These paired lamps have brass and ivory colored metal parts and a glass base. This slightly more transparent jade glass is referred to as Clambroth rather than Jadeite. Singles sell for less than pairs. $75. (pair)

El Mexicano, Morgantown Glass Company, c. 1930s. An abstract pattern with a smooth, but rough appearance. Many years later this pattern was reintroduced in transparent colors and called Crinkle. Ockner" shaped water jug $125, Flat tumblers $9-$15 ea., Shot glass $20, Decanter $180. *(Courtesy of Guy Allen)*

Chapter Twelve
Crystal - A Colorless Glass

Crystal, or clear, is glass that has no color. In the 1800s and early 1900s the majority of all glass produced in America was crystal. But in the early 1920s it began to fall out of favor and colored glass took over the market. Crystal glass continued to have a large market share in the elegant fine glass market even into the 1970s, however for the less expensive everyday Depression glass, a color was often preferred.

The term crystal is often used to describe fine glassware with a high lead content, as in Lead Crystal. This should not be confused with Depression Glass of lesser quality. Lead Crystal has an almost diamond like brilliance and will ring like a bell when tapped. Crystal Depression glass will not have the same ring and has a much duller appearance. Crystal can vary from a brilliant clear to a yellow or gray, depending on the quality of the glass. Sometimes the yellow or gray tint can't be seen until you have the item placed on a bright white tablecloth.

Line #36 cream & sugar, New Martinsville Glass Company, c.1930s. This set has a very elaborate floral cutting that really catches the light. It is part of a full table service. Plates and serving pieces are square in shape with cut off corners, and 4 little points where the corner would have been. Set $35. *(Courtesy of Lucille Fokken)*

Many collectors pass up on the crystal patterns made during the Depression, but I always check them out, as there are many rare items that were only made in crystal. Intermixing crystal items with colored items for dinners is fun. Think of crystal as a neutral color that goes with everything. It is abundant and a good way to begin collecting a full dinnerware set, without spending a lot of money.

Candlewick, Imperial Glass Company, 1936-1984. This is a lovely fan shaped vase with a rich floral cutting. The top and sides are beaded, a design feature on all Candlewick items. $55. *(Courtesy of Anita Tanke)*

Coronet, Fostoria Glass Company, 1939-1960. This crystal pattern is rather plain and only has a ribbon of wave like lines around the very top. This example has a cutting of flowers and plume shaped handles. 3-Part relish $25. *(Courtesy of Lucille Fokken)*

Della Robbia, Westmoreland Glass Company, c. 1920s-1940s. Fruit is the theme on this pattern line. The pressed glass is clear that was stained with red, purple, and yellow colors to accentuate the fruits. Do not pay top dollar for pieces with worn stain. Water Goblet $30 ea.

Florentine #1, "Poppy," Hazel Atlas Glass Company, 1932-1935. This is a sister pattern to Florentine #2, which has a round edge rather than this more scalloped edge. It has a center motif of flowers and scrolls in a pinwheel shape. Tumbler $15, Pitcher $35. *(Courtesy of Lucille Fokken)*

Sandwich, Anchor Hocking Glass Company, c. 1939, 1964-1979. Sandwich is a pattern made by many Depression era glass companies. It received its name by resembling lacey patterns made by the Boston & Sandwich Glass Company of the 1860s. Handled serving tray $25. *(Courtesy of Anita Tanke)*

Early American, Smith Glass Company, 1932-1938. This pattern has a star type pattern in the design and a diamond point background. Was made in milk glass from 1955 to 1965. A full table serve was available. Cup & saucer $10, Bread plate $5, Sherbet $7.

Janice, New Martinsville Glass Company, 1926-1944; Viking Glass Company, 1944-1970. When looking at this pattern I always think of candy corn because of the unique shapes around the bases. Lots of crystal was produced, but light blue is the preferred color to collect. Mosser is currently making this pattern, in cobalt blue and red under the name Nichole. 8.5" Plate $10, Cup & saucer $10, Sugar $12, Creamer $12.

Dancing Nymph, Consolidated Glass Company, 1926-1939. Dancing couples frolic around the edges of this pattern. Highly sought by art deco collectors and never stays in the market long. 10" Plate $85-$95.

Columbia, Federal Glass Company, 1938-1942. Columbia is a crystal pattern with a star center, followed by a ring of bubbles, then rays of graduated bubbles reaching outward. 9.5" Plate $10.

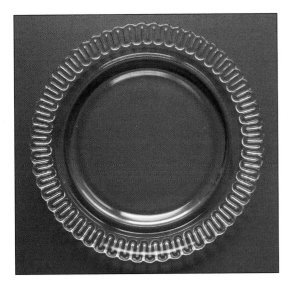

Christmas Candy, Indiana Glass Company, 1937-1950s. As the name suggests, the pattern has a Christmas ribbon candy appearance. 9.5" Dinner plate $10.

Pretzel, Indiana Glass Company, 1930s-1980s. This is a pattern with an extreme design of crossed or X shaped ribs. Plates and bowls sometimes embossed with a fruit design in the center. Creamer $5, Sugar $5, Cup & saucer $7, 11.5" Serving plate $15.

Windsor, "Diamond," Jeanette Glass Company, 1936-1946.
This is a pressed pattern resembling cut glass that consists of a series of diamond shaped facets emanating from a circle of radial ribs. Sugar w/cover $15, Creamer $8.

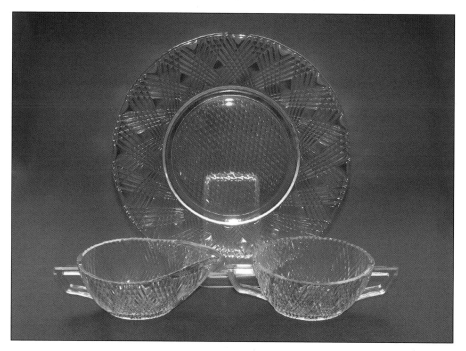

Starlight, Hazel Atlas Glass Company, 1938-1940. A glass pattern that has an open center, then rays of crisscrossing lines going out to the edges. It almost looks like old Hollywood spot lights crossing in the night sky. Sandwich plate $25, Creamer $10, Sugar $15.

Heavy Vertical Rib, Indiana Glass Company, c. 1939. This is a rather heavy pattern but very unique. There are many vertical ribbed patterns, but this has to be the one with the largest ribs. Cream & Sugar $25.

Block Optic, Anchor Hocking Glass Company, 1929-1933. This pattern has a typical 1930s art deco style with wide concentric rings set off in blocks. It is heavy in appearance, yet light and fragile. Tumbler $12, Cup $5.

Heritage, Federal Glass Company, 1940-1955. Heritage is a pattern that really catches the light well. It has a scrolling design with a stippled background. 8" Plate $8, Cup & saucer $7.

Rock Crystal, McKee Glass Company, c. 1920s-1930s. This is a pressed pattern containing flowers and scrolls. Plates were made with scalloped and round edges. 7-Part relish tray $35, Sherbet $14.

Colonial, "Knife and Fork," Hocking Glass Company, 1934-1936. This is a great pattern with rays from the center that reach to a wave in the edge of the design. 6" Plate $7, 4" Cocktail $15.

Ring, "Banded Ring," Hocking Glass Company, 1927-1932. A popular pattern of crystal with bands of concentric molded rings. It is also found decorated with colored bands. Sandwich server $15.

Crystolite, Heisey Glass Company, 1937-1957. This is a vertical rounded rib pattern that is quite heavy. Most of the pieces will be marked with the diamond H logo of Heisey, but not all. Covered Candy $50.

Stars and Stripes, Anchor Hocking Glass Company, 1942. It is a very small line, but one that collectors hunt for. Almost like the Queen Mary pattern, but with eagles in the centers of the plate and stars around all of the pieces. Made to go along with the wave of patriotism at the outbreak of World War II. Sherbet $19.

"S" Pattern, "Stipple Rose Band," MacBeth-Evans Glass Company, 1930-1933. The pattern of this line has a band with a rose in it. The background is stippled in the center. It was made with and without the silver trim. 4" Tumbler $10.

Chapter Thirteen
Sky Blue - A Light Blue

    As the name suggests, Sky Blue is a light, transparent shade that resembles the color of a cloudless sky. This shade of blue can vary from company to company, but is normally consistent throughout a pattern. Companies used many names to refer to it such as Moonlight by Cambridge, Sapphire by Anchor Hocking, Copen by Tiffin, Azure by Fostoria, Madonna by Federal and countless other names. There is also a light opaque blue called Delphite that I should mention. You will not find very much Delphite outside of the kitchenware lines, but there are some Depression Glass patterns in this color.

    Fire-King's Sapphire Blue pattern is a large line of oven ware and kitchenware items that people love to collect. Almost everyone has a pie plate tucked inside his or her cupboard that was passed down from mom or grandma. I still use my Sapphire Blue mixing bowls and measuring cups. They still hold up in the oven, but don't use them in your microwave, as I've broken one this way.

Caprice, Cambridge Glass Company, 1936-1957. An elegant glassware pattern with circular swirls, like ripples in a pond. So many shapes were made in this line that it would take you years to find just half of them. Creamer $25, Sugar $20, Footed bowl $45. *(Courtesy of Marlene McCabe)*

A color just a bit darker than sky blue is Capri. I've included some items in this chapter of this color. It's a rich electric blue and more of a true blue color. Capri is a color that encompasses many pattern lines made by Hazel Atlas in the 1960s. It was extremely popular to collect in the 1980s and 1990s, but demand has since declined. This is partly due to it being harder to find. It's one of those colors that once you have two or three pieces, you just have to find more. It's a light cheery color that is wonderful to use in the summertime.

Mayfair, "Open Rose," Hocking Glass Company, 1931-1937. A very popular pattern with over 50 different items made. The center has a circle of roses with widely spaced lines. 7" Vegetable bowl $65, 12" Deep fruit bowl $115. *(Courtesy of Barb Dalton)*

Feather, Jeanette Glass Company, c. 1950s. This center-handled tray has rays of feathers reaching outward to the edge. This is the perfect tray to use for luncheons and get-togethers. $30. *(Courtesy of Anita Tanke)*

Bubble, Anchor Hocking Glass Company, 1940-1965. Bubble is a very popular and inexpensive pattern to collect. Centers are rayed and the edges have a bubble look. Oval platter $18, Sugar $30, Creamer $40, Dinner plate $10, Cup $15, Saucer $2.

Aunt Polly, U.S. Glass Company, c. 1920s. This is a ribbed pattern with a diamond pattern in the lower part of the design. Sherbet $15.

Empire, Imperial Glass Company, c. mid 1930s. This flower bowl is another of the ribbed patterns that were so popular during the 1930s. This was sold with and without a wire flower frog cage that fit onto the top. $15.

Velva, Tiffin Glass Company, c. 1935-1940s. This pattern is seldom seen and very difficult to find. It can be transparent like this piece or have frosted areas. $35.

Crinkle, Morgantown Glass Company, 1940s –1960s. An abstract pattern with a smooth, but rough appearance. Many items were made in a rainbow of colors. "San Juan" shaped Tankard $55, Footed tumbler $12, Flat tumbler $10. *(Courtesy of Guy Allen)*

Gazebo, Paden City Glass Company, c. 1930s. As the name suggests, this pattern has a Gazebo in it. Gazebo is the name of the etching and not the glass shape itself. The shapes with the teardrop edge without the Gazebo etching are called Vermillion. The heart shaped candy in the center has a larger version of the Gazebo and is called Utopia by collectors. Handled tray $75, Heart candy dish $175, Urn candy $125.

Fire-King Sapphire Blue Oven Glass, Anchor Hocking Glass Company, 1942-1950s. This ovenware was in everyone's home and stood up to lots of use. The line consisted of all kitchenware items in various sizes. Large mixing bowl $25, Custard cup $5, Covered casserole $18.

Covered candy, New Martinsville Glass Company, c. 1930s. This cone-shaped candy dish has a very electric blue color. The only pattern really is an internal panel optic inside the glass. $35.

Comet, Paden City Glass Company, c. 1930s. Comet is the name of this pressed pattern, not the name of the etching. The floral etching is called Hillsboro. $65.

Harp, Jeanette Glass Company, 1954-1957. Here is a beautiful pattern with a musical name. Featuring a harp or lyre, with a dainty all over stippling, even on the base. $45.

Capri, Hazel Ware Division of Continental Can, c. 1960s. Capri is really the term used for the color of blue made at Hazel Ware, and includes several patterns all grouped into one. This vase is in the Dots pattern. 9" Vase $25.

Capri, Hazel Ware Division of Continental Can, c. 1960s. This pattern is called Seashell, another pattern that falls into what has become the Capri line. The snack set is one of my favorites to use at luncheons. Snack plate $12, Cup $9, 5.5" Bowl $8, 8.75" Bowl $20.

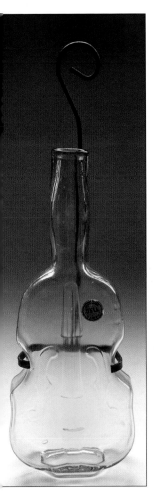

Violin vase, Dell Glass Company, c. 1930s-1940s. This vase is dainty and thin glass in a wire holder for hanging. Sold though the large mail order catalogs, it became widely distributed. $35.

Sunburst, Kemple Glass Company, c. 1950s-1970. The Sunburst pattern is an old pattern first produced by McKee Glass Company. Kemple purchased the molds in the 1950s and reproduced the pattern for many years in various colors. This pattern has a twisted sunburst with crosshatching inside it. $25.

Valencia Waffle, Adams & Company, c. 1885-1890s. This is a very old pattern that I place in this book to show how far back this light blue color was made. This is a water tray with a block and star pattern. $60. *(Courtesy of Guy Allen)*

Chapter Fourteen
Forest Green - The
Emerald Color

This dark, emerald-green color is a holiday favorite. Its rich, deep tone is like no other color. Production of this color was early in the Depression era, and it was produced by most of the American glasshouses of the time. It was not until the 1950s, when Anchor Hocking began marketing its dark green glass under the name Forest Green, that its popularity took off in a big way. The term Forest Green was first used by Cambridge in the early 1930s. It was a slightly lighter green with just a hint of yellow. The name originates from Forest Glass, which was medieval glass made in the forest areas of Northwestern Europe. It was a glass characterized by a variety of greenish-yellow colors.

I do not see many kitchenware items in this dark green color. The first pieces I've purchased were vases, which are found in many shapes and sizes. The most popular pattern was made by Anchor Hocking and is called Charm. It is a square shaped pattern that was made in the early 1950s. Most of the pieces are easy to find and affordable, however never pass on the large dinner plates or platter as they can take years to find.

Bubble, Anchor Hocking Glass Company, 1940-1965. Centers are rayed and the edges have a bubble look. Sugar $14, Creamer $15.

When the calendar flips to December, you'll find my kitchen window sill filled with forest green vases. In the center of my table I use the largest, filled with white flowers. As the holidays approach, the table is set with more green glass. The Charm pattern was made in Forest Green and Ruby Red, which I intermix for a wonderful festive look.

Burple, Anchor Hocking Glass Company, c. 1940s and later. A very attractive dessert set with rows of a beaded effect, swirled lines, and footed. The set is ideal for a festive holiday setting. 8.5" Bowl $20, 4.5" Bowl $8.

Glades, Paden City Glass Company, c. 1930s. This pattern is art deco with vertical ribs on the sides. These cocktail glasses have a corset shape that is unique. $25 ea.

Boppie, Anchor Hocking Glass Company, 1940-1965. This was a stem line created to sell with the Bubble pattern. The bowls are a forest green while the beaded feet are in crystal glass. 5.5oz Goblet $12, 9.5oz Goblet $13.

Spice shakers, Owens-Illinois Glass Company, c. 1930s-1940s. These shakers have a ribbed pattern on the top and plain bottoms. The covers have a cover to keep moisture out. $5 ea. *(Courtesy of Guy Allen)*

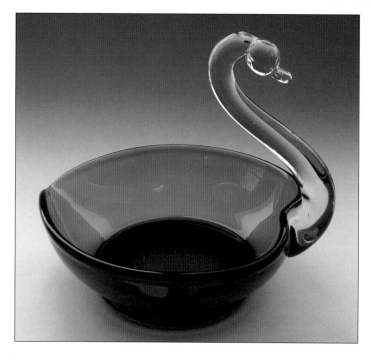

Swan candy dish, New Martinsville & Viking Glass Company, 1940-1960. This little gem has a green body, crystal neck, and is referred to as the "Sweetheart" shape. During the holidays it begs to hold some hard candy. $25-$30.

Swan table set, New Martinsville & Viking Glass Company, 1940-1960. This set of swans is quite stunning together. The candleholders are the same as the candy dish in the previous photo, only with a socket in the base. They too are in the "Sweetheart" shape. Candleholders $30-$35 ea, Large Swan $75-$85. *(Courtesy of Anita Tanke)*

Waterford, "Waffle," Hocking Glass Company, (Crystal 1938-1944), (Forest Green 1950s). A great relish tray with a forest green tray and milk glass inserts. Waterford has a diagonal block pattern its edges. Set $55.

Pineapple & Hoover vases, Anchor Hocking Glass Company, 1950-1967. On the left is the Pineapple vase, called that because of the shape. One the right is the Hoover with its scalloped top collar. Pineapple $15, Hoover $20.

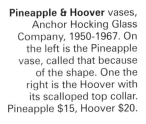

Moon powder jar, Paden City Glass Company, c. 1930s. This covered jar has an emerald green cover and a crystal bottom. It is a pressed pattern of diamonds and was sold with matching perfume bottles. $35.

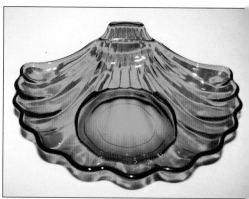

Fan dish, Anchor Hocking Glass Company, c. 1950s. This is a wonderful little nappy in the shape of a shell. On one side is a handle to pass it with. $12. *(Courtesy of Guy Allen)*

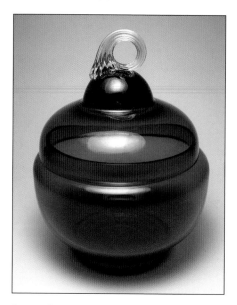

Reeded, "Spun," Imperial Glass Company, c. 1936-1960s. Fine vertical ribbing, over the entire surface define this pattern. Many colors and items were made. Pitcher $75, Tumbler $10. *(Courtesy of Guy Allen)*

Covered candy, Fostoria Glass Company, 1934-1942. This is a high quality blown glass dish with a crystal handle. Empire Green was the name used by Fostoria for this dark green. $125.

Moondrops, New Martinsville Glass Company, 1932-1940s. A very complete pattern of numerous unique items made in various vibrant colors. Very art deco in style with fan shaped stoppers and finals. Shot glass $10, Decanter $50. (*Courtesy of Guy Allen*)

Fire-King Charm, Anchor Hocking Glass Company, 1950-1954. Charm is a wonderful pattern with square plates, cups, and bowls. This photo shows how festive a table full of forest green glass can look. Happy hunting!

Chapter Fifteen
Ruby Red - A Festive Color

Ruby red is a bright color that immediately invokes thoughts of the winter holidays. It is a shade that not all companies manufactured. Depression era patterns made in red are scarce and expensive when they do surface. Red glass made later in the 1950s is much easier to find and more affordable to collect.

Red glass was first developed in the 1890s by the Kopp Glass Company of Swissvale, Pennsylvania. Kopp was first to develop a deep intense red glass using selenium. This red glass was then, and still is, favored by the railroad industry for making signaling lights. You can still see examples of Kopp's selenium red every time you sit at a traffic light.

Royal Ruby, Anchor Hocking Glass Company, c. 1938-1960s. This is a plain pattern, but because of the rich red color, it remains simple and elegant. The name Royal Ruby should only be used to describe glass made by Anchor Hocking. (left to right) 3qt. Tilt Pitcher $45, 42 oz. Upright Pitcher $45, 5oz. Tumbler $6.50, 9oz. Tumbler $7.50, 3.5 oz. Tumbler $12.50 *(Courtesy of Meg Canepa)*

The largest manufacturer of red glass has to be the Anchor Hocking Glass Company. They marketed their red glass under the name Royal Ruby, a name referring to the color, not the pattern. Many sellers refer to all red glass as Royal Ruby, but it really should only be used to describe Anchor Hocking's patterns. Royal Ruby was very popular all through the 1940s and 1950s. Many of the patterns were made in both Royal Ruby and Forest Green colors, which are wonderful colors to intermix in a table setting.

For holiday festivities decorating with ruby red glass is phenomenal! I bring mine out in early December and again on Valentines Day.

Royal Ruby, Anchor Hocking Glass Company, c. 1938-1960s. Salad plate $5, Dinner plate $11, Cup $8, saucer $3.50, Sugar $8, Creamer $8, Bowl $12, Sherbet $9.50 *(Courtesy of Meg Canepa)*

Royal Ruby, Anchor Hocking Glass Company, c. 1938-1960s. (left to right) "Wilson" 4" fancy edge ball vase $8, 9" "Hoover" vase $20, 4" "Wilson" plain edge $7.50, 6.5" "Harding" vase $9. *(Courtesy of Meg Canepa)*

Royal Ruby, Anchor Hocking Glass Company, c. 1938-1960s. Salad bowl $30, Smaller berry bowl $25. *(Courtesy of Meg Canepa)*

Royal Ruby, Anchor Hocking Glass Company, c. 1938-1960s. 3 Styles of vases $9 ea.

Royal Ruby, Anchor Hocking Glass Company, c. 1938-1960s. Tilt ball shaped water jug with a swirl pattern. $40.

Bubble, Anchor Hocking Glass Company, 1940-1965. Rows of bubbles flow up the sides of this pattern. Water pitcher $65, Tall tumbler $16, low tumbler $10.

Coronation, "Banded Rib," Hocking Glass Company, 1936-1940. This pattern is famous for its berry bowl set that was manufactured for a "Special Sales" promotion. The open handles make this set very attractive. 8" Bowl $20, 4.25" Bowl $9.50.

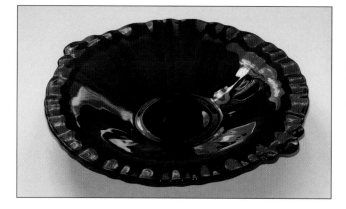

Old Cafe, Hocking Glass Company, 1936-1940. This ruby red candy dish $20.

Sandwich, Indiana Glass Company, (Red 1933). This is a very attractive bowl with a sunflower and scroll design. 5.5" Bowl $15.

Crow's Foot, Paden City Glass Company, c. 1930s. This pattern can have a square or round shape; both are considered to be Crow's Foot. The pattern has four rows of teardrops followed by a fan shaped feature that looks almost like a bird track. Serving Tray $70. *(Courtesy of Marlene McCabe)*

Glades, Paden City Glass Company, c. 1930s. This pattern is art deco with vertical ribs on the sides. Creamer & Sugar $45.

Lace Edge, "Katy," Imperial Glass Company, c. 1930s. The Lace Edge line has an open lace edge and a diamond hatched pattern on the sides. $30.

#717, Candy jar, Imperial Glass Company, c. 1930s. This 6-sided candy jar is about 7 inches tall and has a unique shape. It was made in many colors. $50.

#1007 Flowerlite, Viking Glass Company, c. 1951-1973. This footed round vase holds a flower frog with a candle socket on the top. Footed candleholders like this are called Flowerlites. $65. (Complete w/frog)

Hobnail, Fenton Art Glass Company, c.1950s. This is a deep red candle with a hobnail design, and crimped top. $25. *(Courtesy Linda Wasko)*

Fenton Art Glass Company, c. 1950s. This is a small pressed glass swan dish with great detail. The compote is in the **Thumbnail** pattern, which was made for many years in various colors. Swan $20, Compote $25.

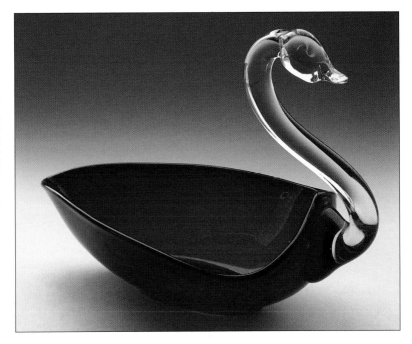

Pall Mall swan, Duncan Miller Glass Company, c. 1945. The dish of this swan is a deep shade of red accented by a crystal clear neck. $55.

Franklin, Fenton Art Glass Company, c. 1934-1940. A very unique decanter set that is art deco in style. The Franklin line only contained a decanter and four tumblers of various sizes. 6-pc set $175.

Chapter Sixteen
Milk Glass - An Opaque White

Milk Glass is a term referring to an opaque glass that is basically the color of milk. It's an early color originating in Venice during the 16th century. In America it was made by all of the major glass manufactures. In the 1800s it was called opal and used extensively for lampshades, smoke bells and vases. It was not until the 1930s that full dinnerware lines were being made in the white color, but even then, the color was not as popular as the transparent colors being made. Referring to this white glass as "Milk Glass" began in the late 1940s and 1950s when it had an explosion of popularity. This explosion lasted into the 1970's before demand slipped away.

There are some big differences in the old opal glass verses later milk glass. The easiest way to see the difference is to hold it up to a strong light. An old piece will show a glowing orange edge, while the new glass will remain opaque white right out to the rim. Many collectors refer to this as "Looking for the Fire."

Beaded Edge, Westmoreland Glass Company, 1930s-1950s. This milk glass line is quite spectacular when decorated with hand painted fruits or flowers. Shapes are rather plain, with a beaded edge. 7" Salad plate $15 (strawberries), 10.5" Dinner plate $40 (cherries), Tumbler $12. (red edge).

Values are much higher for the older glass and there is far less available in the marketplace. The milk glass of the 1950s, 60s, and 70s is still quite abundant and affordable. Just go to any garage sale and you are likely to find a piece or two before your first cup of coffee is gone.

My first piece of milk glass was a console set in the Paneled Grape pattern made by Westmoreland. The stark whiteness of the glass really sets off any fruit or candy I place in the bowl. It's a color that intermixes well with just about any other glass color and was often marketed that way by the glass companies. My forest green Waterford pattern relish with its milk glass inserts is always a head turner at holiday parties.

Petalware, MacBeth-Evans Glass Company, 1930-1950. This pattern with its petal like edges is wonderful. It has an opalescent appearance not by an added color, but rather by thin and thicker areas of glass. Decorated 9" dinner plate $20, Decorated 6" sherbet plate $5.

Hobnail, Fenton Art Glass Company, 1939-1980s. This is beautiful and functional glass basket with a hobnail pattern on the underside. An applied handle crimped edge at to its allure. $75. *(Courtesy of Gloria Nelson)*

#103 compote, Imperial Glass Company, 1950s. This is a great piece of glass with molded leaves on its base and beads or balls around the top edge. Some consider this part of the Candlewick line, but because of the leaves, most do not. It is 9.5 inches wide and stands 5.75 inches tall. $25.

Thumbprint, Westmoreland Glass Company, c. 1950s-1960s. Westmoreland refers to this covered dish as a honey dish. It has a thumbprint design on the cover and base. It is also decorated with a hand painted decoration called Roses and Bows. $35. *(Courtesy of Marlene McCabe)*

Lacy Dewdrop, Kemple Glass Company, 1946-1970. This is a very old pattern originally done by Co-Operative Flint Glass Company, then Phoenix Glass Company, and finally Kemple. The pattern contains little beads around a teardrop and oval shape shapes. $15.

Betsy Ross, Fostoria Glass Company, c. 1954-1965. This pattern is called Betsy Ross when it is milk glass; crystal is earlier and is called Wistar. It has open areas around an ivy leaf design. $25 (pair).

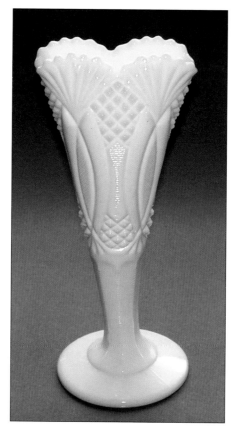

Heritage, Smith Glass Company, 1961-1965. This tall white vase is thick glass so very stable for flowers. It was made from an old McKee mold from their Jubilee line. The pattern has a fan and zipper design. $25.

Hobnail, Fenton Art Glass Company, 1961-1985. This is beautiful pattern with hobnails or dots covering the outside. Candlesticks $35 (pair), Ruffled bowl $30.

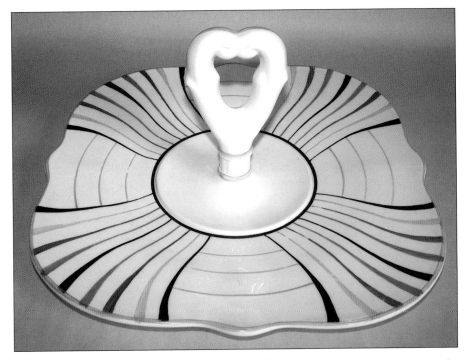

Crow's Foot, Paden City Glass Company, c. 1930s. This pattern can have a square or round shape; both are considered to be Crow's Foot. The pattern has four rows of teardrops followed by a fan shaped feature that looks almost like a bird track. This is a very rare pattern to find in white glass. Center handled server $95.

Vitrock, Hocking Glass Company, 1934-1937. Vitrock is a very unappreciated pattern that I find lovely. It has plain centers with a molded flower edge. 8.75" Luncheon plate $5, 10" Dinner plate $10, Cream soup bowl $15.

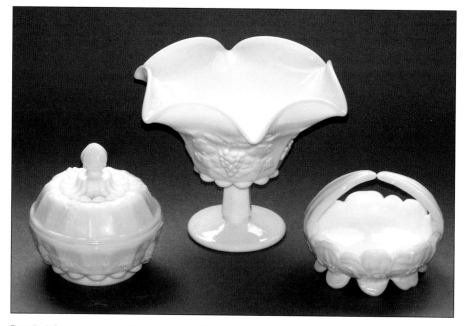

Paneled Grape / Pansy, Westmoreland Glass Company, c. 1950s-1970s. This pattern is white with decorations. It is an extremely large line with over one hundred shapes made. The grape pattern design stand out to make it distinctive. On the far right is a basket in the Pansy pattern. Its handles curve up but do not tough. Puff box or jelly $27.50, Footed 6" bowl $30, Pansy basket $18.

Silver Crest, Fenton Art Glass Company, 1943-1980s. This pattern is one of Fenton's longest production lines. There are many dates of the pieces produced. Opal was the white before 1958 and had opalescence when held to light. In 1958 it was changed to milk glass, which was very white. Pieces produced after 1973 were signed Fenton. Pieces are almost always crimped on the top giving a very lacy appearance. Candlesticks $25 (pair), Footed bowl $65.

Bibliography

Barnett, Jerry. *Paden City, The Color Company.* Independently published, 1978.

Coe, Randy and Debbie. *Elegant Glass: Early, Depression, and Beyond.* Atglen, Pennsylvania: Schiffer Publishing Ltd., 2007.

Edwards, Bill and Mike Carwile, *Standard Encyclopedia of Pressed Glass.* Paducah, Kentucky: Collector Books, 2005.

Felt, Tom and Elaine & Rich Stoer. *The Glass Candlestick Book Volume 1:* Paducah, Kentucky: Collector Books, 2003.

Felt, Tom and Elaine & Rich Stoer. *The Glass Candlestick Book Volume 2:* Paducah, Kentucky: Collector Books, 2003.

Felt, Tom and Elaine & Rich Stoer. *The Glass Candlestick Book Volume 1.* Paducah, Kentucky: Collector Books, 2005.

Florence, Cathy and Gene. *Collectable Glassware from the 40s 50s 60s.* Paducah, Kentucky: Collector Books, 2005.

Florence, Gene. *Elegant Glassware of the Depression Era.* Paducah, Kentucky: Collector Books, 2003.

Florence, Gene. *Kitchen Glassware of the Depression Year.* Paducah, Kentucky: Collector Books, 2001.

Florence, Gene. *Collector's Encyclopedia of Depression Glass.* Paducah, Kentucky: Collector Books, 2006.

Gallagher, Jerry. *A Handbook of Old Morgantown Glass.* Independently published, 1995.

Garmon, Lee and Dick Spencer. *Glass Animals of the Depression Era.* Paducah, Kentucky: Collector Books, 1993.

Goshe, Ed, Ruth Hemminger, and Leslie Pina. *Tiffin Depression Era Stems & Tableware.* Atglen, Pennsylvania: Schiffer Publishing Ltd., 1998.

Hicks, Joyce. *Just Jenkins.* Independently published, 1988.

Jenks, Bill and Jerry Luna. *Early American Pattern Glass 1850-1910.* Radnor, Pennsylvania: Wallace-Homestead Book Company, 1990.

Keller, Joe and David Ross. *Jadite, An Identification & Price Guide.* Atglen, Pennsylvania: Schiffer Publishing Ltd., 1999.

Kovar, Lorraine. *Westmoreland Glass 1950-1984.* Volume 1. Marietta, Ohio: Antique Publications, 1991.

Kovar, Lorraine. *Westmoreland Glass 1950-1984.* Volume 2. Marietta, Ohio: Antique Publications, 1991.

Kovar, Lorraine. *Westmoreland Glass 1950-1984.* Volume 3. Marietta, Ohio: Antique Publications, 1997.

Long, Milbra and Emily Seate. *Fostoria Tableware, 1924-1943, The Crystal For America.* Paducah, Kentucky: Collector Books, 1999.

Long, Milbra and Emily Seate. *Fostoria Useful and Ornamental, The Crystal For America.* Paducah, Kentucky: Collector Books, 2000.

Mauzy, Jim and Barbara. *Mauzy's Comprehensive Handbook of Depression Glass Prices.* Atglen, Pennsylvania: Schiffer Publishing Ltd., 2003.

Measell, James. *New Martinsville Glass, 1900-1944.* Marietta, Ohio: Antique Publications, 1994.

Measell, James and Berry Wiggins. *Great American Glass of the Roaring 20s & Depression Era.* Book 1. Marietta, Ohio: Antique Publications, 1998.

Measell, James and Berry Wiggins. *Great American Glass of the Roaring 20s & Depression Era.* Book 2. Marietta, Ohio: Antique Publications, 2000.

Pina, Leslie and Jerry Gallagher. *Tiffin Glass, 1914-1940.* Atglen, Pennsylvania: Schiffer Publishing Ltd., 1996.

Six, Dean. *West Virginia Glass Between the World Wars.* Atglen, Pennsylvania: Schiffer Publishing Ltd., 2002.

Schmidt, Tim. *Central Glass Works, The Depression Era.* Atglen, Pennsylvania: Schiffer Publishing Ltd., 2004.

Walker, William, Melissa Bratkovich, and Joan Walker. *Paden City Glass Company.* Marietta, Ohio: Antique Publications, 2003.

Weatherman, Hazel Marie. *Colored Glassware of the Depression Era 2.* Springfield, Missouri: Weatherman Glass Books, 1974.

Whitmyer, Margaret and Kenn. *Fenton Art Glass, Identification and Value Guide.* Paducah, Kentucky: Collector Books, 1996.

Wilson, Jack. *Phoenix & Consolidated Art Glass 1926-1980.* Marietta, Ohio: Antique Publications, 1989.

Wilson, Chas West. *Westmoreland Glass, Identification and Value Guide.* Paducah, Kentucky: Collector Books, 1996.

Yeske, Doris. *Depression Glass, Dinnerware Accessories.* Atglen, Pennsylvania: Schiffer Publishing Ltd., 2005.

Index of Pattern Names & Makers

7-Piece Beverage Set, Tiffin Glass Company, 55
#36 Cream & Sugar, New Martinsville Glass Company, 126
#103 Compote, Imperial Glass Company, 164
#323 Loaf cream and sugar, Paden City Glass Company, 22
581 Candleholders, Anchor Hocking Glass Company, 91
#894, Lancaster Glass Company, 58
#1007 Flowerlite, Viking Glass Company, 160
#2002 Serving Bowl, Central Glass Works, 97

Adam, Jeannette Glass Company, 23
American Beauty Rose, Imperial Glass Company, 116
Ardith, Paden City Glass Company, 28, 98
Aunt Polly, U.S. Glass Company, 142
Aurora, Hazel-Atlas Glass Company, 74
Avocado, "Sweet Pear," Indiana Glass Company, 13, 31

Balda, Central Glass Works, 47, 94
Baroque, Fostoria Glass Company, 53
Basket Weave with Open Edge, Fenton Art Glass Company, 66
Beaded Block, Imperial Glass Company, 69
Beaded Edge, Westmoreland Glass Company, 162
Bel-aire, Imperial Glass Company, 56, 105
Betsy Ross, Fostoria Glass Company, 165
Betty Mae Decanter Set, Paden City Glass Company, 38
Black Forest, Paden City Glass Company, 39
Block Optic, Anchor Hocking Glass Company, 44, 135
Blossoms and Palms, Northwood Glass Company, 62
Boppie, Anchor Hocking Glass Company, 149
Bowknot, Maker unknown, 43
Bubble, Anchor Hocking Glass Company, 141, 148, 157
Burple, Anchor Hocking Glass Company, 149

Cable Flute, Lancaster Glass Company, 57
Camellia, Jeannette Glass Company, 115
Cameo, "Ballerina," Hocking Glass Company, 35, 49
Candlewick, Imperial Glass Company, 102, 127
Candy Dish, Fostoria Glass Company, 99

Candy Jar, Imperial Glass Company, 159
Cane Landrum, "Shape #765," Lancaster Glass Company, 57
Canterbury, Duncan & Miller, 68
Capri, " Dots," Hazel Ware Division of Continental Can, 146
Capri, "Seashell," Hazel Ware Division of Continental Can, 146
Caprice, Cambridge Glass Company, 139
Catalonian, Consolidated Lamp and Glass Company, 94
Chanticleer, Duncan & Miller Glass Company, 80
Charade, Diamond Glass Company, 105
Cherry Blossom, Jeannette Glass Company, 10
Christmas Candy, Indiana Glass Company, 133
Circled Scroll, Dugan Glass Company, 1, 117
Cloverleaf, Hazel-Atlas Glass Company, 30, 58, 100
Coin Dot, Fenton Art Glass Company, 68
Colonial, "Knife and Fork," Hocking Glass Company, 137
Columbia, Federal Glass Company, 132
Comet, Paden City Glass Company, 145
Console Set, Tiffin Glass Company, 50
Coral, Jefferson Glass Company, 69
Coronation, "Banded Rib," Hocking Glass Company, 157
Coronet, Fostoria Glass Company, 128
Covered Candy, Fostoria Glass Company, 152
Covered Candy, New Martinsville Glass Company, 145
Crinkle, Morgantown Glass Company, 90, 143
Crow's Foot, Paden City Glass Company, 5, 40, 76, 158, 167
Crystolite, Heisey Glass Company, 138
Cupid, Fostoria Glass Company, 99
Cupid, Paden City Glass Company, 28

Daisy, Indiana Glass Company, 88
Dancing Nymph, Consolidated Glass Company, 132
Decanter Set, Fostoria Glass Company, 89
Deco Fan, Central Glass Works, 76
Della Robbia, Westmoreland Glass Company, 129
Diamond Block, "Little Jewel," Imperial Glass Company, 32
Diamond Quilted, Imperial Glass Company, 15
Diamond Rib Vase, Fenton Art Glass Company, 118
Diana, Federal Glass Company, 81
Dogwood, "Apple Blossom," MacBeth-Evans Glass Company, 19
Doric, Jeannette Glass Company, 17

Early American, Smith Glass Company, 130
Egg Harbor, Liberty Works, 37
El Mexicano, Morgantown Glass Company, 125
El Rancho, Bryce Glass Company, 80, 90

Empire, Imperial Glass Company, 142
Empress, Heisey Glass Company, 52

Fan Dish, Anchor Hocking Glass Company, 152
Fan Vase, Central Glass Works, 96
Feather, Jeanette Glass Company, 140
Fine Rib Ball Pitcher, Hazel-Atlas Glass Company, 75
Finger Bowl & Under Plate, Steuben Glass Works, 124
Fire-King Batter Pitcher, Anchor Hocking Glass Corporation, 121
Fire-King Charm, Anchor Hocking Glass Company, 153
Fire-King Mixing Bowls, Anchor Hocking Corporation, 122
Fire-King Peach Lustre, Anchor Hocking Glass Corporation, 119
Fire-King Restaurant Ware Cups, Anchor Hocking Corporation, 122
Fire-King Restaurant Ware Place Setting, Anchor Hocking Corporation, 121
Fire-King Sapphire Blue Oven Glass, Anchor Hocking Glass Company, 144
Fire-King Shell, "Regency Shell," Anchor Hocking Glass Corporation, 123
Fire-King Skillet, Anchor Hocking Glass Corporation, 124
Fish Canapé Trays, Imperial Glass Company, 79
Floragold, "Louisa," Jeanette Glass Company, 176, 113
Floral and Diamond Band, U.S. Glass Company, 35
Florentine #1, "Poppy," Hazel Atlas Glass Company, 129
Florentine #2, "Poppy," Hazel-Atlas Glass Company, 53
Florentine, Cambridge Glass Company, 37
Flower Bowl, Beaumont Tumbler Company, 103
Flower Garden With Butterflies, U.S. Glass Company, 16, 101, 111
Fountain Line, Jenkins Glass Company, 41
Frances, Central Glass Company, 16
Franklin, Fenton Art Glass Company, 161

Gazebo, Paden City Glass Company, 144
Geneva Powder Jar, New Martinsville Glass Company, 25
Georgian, "Lovebirds," Federal Glass Company, 36
Georgian, Duncan & Miller Glass Company, 77
Glades, Paden City Glass Company, 80, 149, 159
Glass Utility Bowl, Federal Glass Company, 84
Golf Ball, Morgantown Glass Company, 110, 111

Harp, Jeanette Glass Company, 146
Heavy Vertical Rib, Indiana Glass Company, 135
Heirloom, Fostoria Glass Company, 63
Heritage, Federal Glass Company, 136
Heritage, Smith Glass Company, 166

Hobnail Opalescent, Fenton Art Glass Company, 64, 67
Hobnail, Fenton Art Glass Company, 4, 160, 163, 166
Holly, "Holly and Berries," Fenton Art Glass Company, 116
Honey Bee Candy Box, Indiana Glass Company for Tiara Exclusives, 108
Hoover Vase, Anchor Hocking Glass Company, 151
Horseshoe, "No. 612," Indiana Glass Company, 47

Ice Buckets, Fostoria Glass Company, 93
Iris, "Iris and Herringbone," Jeanette Glass Company, 114

Jane Ray, Anchor Hocking Glass Corporation, 123
Janice, New Martinsville Glass Company, 131
Jolly Bear, Jefferson Glass Company, 70
Jubilee, Lancaster Glass Company, 22, 54
Jumbo Ashtray, L.E. Smith Glass Company / Greensburg Glass Works, 104

Kirby, Morgantown Glass Company, 109

Lace Edge, "Genie", Imperial Glass Company, 63
Lace Edge, "Katy," Imperial Glass Company, 86, 159
Lacy Dewdrop, Kemple Glass Company, 165
Lamps, Houzex Glass Company, 125
Lattice Medallion, Northwood Glass Company, 59
Leaf and Diamond, Jefferson Glass Company, 60
Lincoln Inn, Fenton Art Glass Company, 79
Lorain, "Basket," Indiana Glass Company, 48

Madrid, Federal Glass Company, 85
Manhattan, "Horizontal Ribbed," Anchor Hocking Glass Company, 18
Many Loops, Jefferson Glass Company, 61
Mayfair, "Open Rose," Hocking Glass Company, 20, 21, 46, 140
Mayfair, Fostoria Glass Company, 19, 52
Miss America, Hocking Glass Company, 7
Modernistic, New Martinsville Glass Company, 103
Moderntone, Hazel-Atlas Glass Company, 72, 73
Moon Powder Jar, Paden City Glass Company, 152
Moondrops, New Martinsville Glass Company, 78, 153
Moonstone, Anchor Hocking Glass Company, 65
Moroccan Amethyst, "Square," Hazel Ware - Division of Continental Can, 91
Moroccan Amethyst, "Swirl," Hazel Ware - Division of Continental Can, 90
Mt. Pleasant, L. E. Smith Glass Company, 100

NewBound, Imperial Glass Company, 109
Normandy, "Bouquet & Lace," Federal Glass Company, 83, 115
Notched Square, Liberty Works, 29

Oakleaf, Fostoria Glass Company, 99
Old Cafe, Hocking Glass Company, 158
Old Colony, "Open Lace," Hocking Glass Company, 8, 9
Old Sandwich, Heisey Glass Company, 51
Orchid, Paden City Glass Company, 87
Ovide, Hazel Atlas Glass Company, 95
Oyster & Pearl, Anchor Hocking Glass Company, 1, 26, 27

Pall Mall Swan, Duncan Miller Glass Company, 1, 161
Palm Leaf, Fostoria Glass Company, 115
Paneled Grape, Westmoreland Glass Company, 168
Pansy, Westmoreland Glass Company, 168
Patrician, Federal Glass Company, 83
Peacock & Wild Rose, Paden City Glass Company, 97
Pebbled Rim, "Melba," L.E. Smith Glass Company, 45
Petalware, MacBeth-Evans Glass Company, 163
Pineapple Vase, Anchor Hocking Glass Company, 151
Plymouth, Fenton Art Glass Company, 106
Pretzel, Indiana Glass Company, 133
Princess, Hocking Glass Company, 34
Princess, Viking Glass Company, 92
Pump and Trough, Northwood Glass Company, 70

Radiance, New Martinsville Glass Company, 87
Range Set, Jeanette Glass Company, 120
Reeded, "Spun," Imperial Glass Company, 152
Regal, Northwood Glass Company, 61
Ring, "Banded Ring," Hocking Glass Company, 114, 137
Rock Crystal, McKee Glass Company, 137
Rose Cameo, Belmont Tumbler Company, 43
Rosemary, "Dutch Rose," Federal Glass Company, 13, 82
Roxana, Hazel-Atlas Glass Company, 49
Royal Lace, Hazel-Atlas Glass Company, 74
Royal Ruby "Swirl," Anchor Hocking Glass Company, 157
Royal Ruby, "Vases," Hocking Glass Company, 155, 156
Royal Ruby, Anchor Hocking Glass Company, 154, 155
Ruffles and Rings, Northwood Glass Company, 70
Rustic Rib Vase, Fenton Art Glass Company, 118

"S" Pattern, "Stipple Rose Band," MacBeth-Evans Glass Company, 138
Sandwich, Anchor Hocking Glass Company, 129

Sandwich, Indiana Glass Company for Tiara Exclusives, 1, 88
Sandwich, Indiana Glass Company, 158
Shaeffer, Imperial Glass Company, 110
Shamrock Nut Bowls, Indiana Glass Company, for Colony, 110
Sharon, "Cabbage Rose," Federal Glass Company, 14, 84
Shirley Temple Pitcher, Hazel-Atlas Glass Company, 73
Sierra, "Pinwheel," Jeannette Glass Company, 11, 46
Silver Crest, Fenton Art Glass Company, 168
Spartan, Fostoria Glass Company, 93
Spice Shakers, Owens-Illinois Glass Company, 150
Spiral, Hocking Glass Company, 32
Starlight, Hazel Atlas Glass Company, 134
Stars and Stripes, Anchor Hocking Glass Company, 138
Sunburst, Kemple Glass Company, 1, 147
Sunflower, Jeannette Glass Company, 24, 42
Sunkist Reamer, McKee Glass Company, 124
Swan Bowl, Dugan Glass Company, 41
Swan Candy Dish, New Martinsville & Viking Glass Company, 150
Swan Dish, Fenton Art Glass Company, 160
Swan Table Set, New Martinsville & Viking Glass Company, 151
Swirl, "Petal Swirl," Jeanette Glass Company, 107
Swirl, Northwood Glass Company, 115

Tea Room, Indiana Glass Company, 17, 33
Thumbnail, Fenton Art Glass Company, 160
Thumbprint, Westmoreland Glass Company, 164
Tulip, Dell Glass Company, 92
Twisted Optic, Imperial Glass Company, 23
Two-Tone Bud Vase, Huntington Tumbler Company, 3, 79

Utility Bowl, Hazel-Atlas Glass Company, 75

Valencia Waffle, Adams & Company, 147
Vases, Central Glass Works, 94
Vases, Louie Glass Company, 102
Velva, Tiffin Glass Company, 143
Violin Vase, Dell Glass Company, 1, 147
Vitrock, Hocking Glass Company, 167

Waterford Waffle, Hocking Glass Company, 12, 151
Wide Rib, Fenton Art Glass Company, 96
Windmill, "Double Dutch," Imperial Glass Company, 117
Windsor, "Diamond," Jeanette Glass Company, 134

Yorktown, Federal Glass Company, 55, 119